GRANT WRITING

BIDOISM

Est. 2018

for
Grassroots
Organizations and
Nonprofit Leaders

JACQUELEEN M. BIDO, EDD

For information contact:
Bidioism LLC
Email: ceo@bidoism.com
Website: www.bidoism.com
Book and Cover design by Jacqueleen Bido

ISBN: 979-8-9898904-0-8

First Edition: January 25, 2025

DEDICATION

To Tobias A. Fox, Founder and Managing Director of Newark Science and Sustainability, Inc. for

trusting and supporting me through the highs and lows of grant writing.

To the many Grassroots Organizations and Nonprofit Leaders

doing everything in their power to make the world a better place for us all.

To the current and forthcoming grant writers may your gifts be amplified by this book.

To my children Cristina, Alecc, Aleccia, Mackaiyah, and Mackennah remember to

always give back to your community any way you can.

#wholeteamwinning

TABLE OF CONTENTS

BIDOISM:

1. A philosophy to provide "A Strategy for Peace of Mind" and "Authenticity.

ACKNOWLEDGEMENTS

I want to thank God for the daily evolution of this calling. I want to thank Tobias A. Fox, Founder and Managing Director of Newark Science and Sustainability, Inc. for letting me come on this amazing journey of community impact to bring forth "Generational Sustainability". We have transcended the no's and non-believers to bring to fruition something amazing in the City of Newark, Dominican Republic, and beyond. To the Grassroots Organizations I have had the honor to work with, I thank you for all you do that goes underfunded and under acknowledged, yet, is the catalyst to addressing the needs of the community. To the Nonprofit Leaders who bring their vision to life daily against all odds because your mission changes how we see each other and how we see the world. To the funders who have transitioned the request for proposals and areas of funding focus to be more inclusive which offers an opportunity for those doing the greatest impact to be sustained. I thank the stakeholders that come together to make a collective impact understanding there is room for everyone to play a role in making the world a better place. To my children who have watched me spend countless hours in front of my computer, in meetings, typing, traveling, etc. thank you for being there cheering me on.

FORWARD

When how you see it matters!

I was on Facebook January 20, 2014, and read a post that said "Annual Sustainability Conference". I wanted to know more and reached out to the person who posted it. It seems like it was yesterday when I asked "How could I be a speaker for your event?" At that time the event was still being logistically organized. The initial conversation went into discussing some of the things I was involved in, especially since at the time Newark Public School District was under state control and the community was mobilizing to address the inequalities that existed. He shared my post about it and I thanked him and he said:

> Tobias: "I'm only playing my part"
>
> Bido: "Well that is all I want all of us to do"

Time passed and again I saw a post from Tobias and this time it spoke to obtaining his 501c3 for Newark Science and Sustainability, Inc. (Newark SaS) I reached out again and said:

> Bido: "Congrats on the 501c3 should you need any help... I can offer... Please do not hesitate to ask..."

At this time I still did not formally know Tobias A. Fox who posted the comment and I also did not know how this post would be the foundation for friendship that would be the catalyst to a host of grassroots impact throughout the City of Newark, NJ, the State of New Jersey and abroad in Constanza, Dominican Republic and beyond.

Throughout that year we communicated back and forth about different things dealing with Newark Science and Sustainability, Inc. One day I asked if we could collaborate on the development of a garden. He educated me on the Adopt-a-Lot program that existed in the City of Newark. For $1 dollar you could lease an abandoned lot for a year and beautify it via a garden, art, or other form of green space. At the time I had just moved to Orlando, Fl and flew in to search for the perfect lot. I came upon the final lot on the list and it was located on Fairmount Ave. This lot was truly abandoned in every sense of the word trash, glass from beer bottles, and a host of things that were unsightly. I let Tobias know and so it began. The name of the garden would be "The Garden of Hope". Neither one of us could have imagined that this location would ultimately become the future Headquarters for Newark Science and Sustainability, Inc.

The first grant I won with Newark SaS was for the Garden of Hope in Newark, New Jersey. It was a Green Thumb grant for $2000 at the time when we found out we felt like we hit the grant lottery. That grant came with a tools package for gardening along with the money. We created a needs list and I wrote a newsletter sharing it. Immediately we received help from the community to fulfill the need. We even had a gentleman reach out and told us that he would repaint the mural on the lot and all we needed to do was supply the paint. We put raised beds, benches, and positive sayings all around. The Garden of Hope was transformed. In the years to follow I kept writing grants and we kept feeling like we won the lottery. The mission of Newark SaS was coming to life with every program and event. Tobias and I over the years prioritized the people in everything we did. Anyone who joined interned would understand our mission and the 5 Pillars to impact the community in their own way. We collaborated with companies, local urban farmers and growers, highschool interns, college interns, community members, universities, from our youth to our elders, everyone has been a part of the journey. We pride ourselves on "Generational Sustainability".

This book is written to first inspire other people and organizations to understand that "how you see it matters." If on the day Tobias and I saw the lot we did not see beyond what was before us there would be no Garden of Hope. Second, the grant writing process is only as successful as the mission, the programming, and above all the impact you seek to have on the people for the people. It is written for the Funders. That this book affirms your continued support of the work that changes lives locally, regionally, nationally, and globally. It is written for the reader. That this book affirms and supports your calling, mission or vision to be a positive proponent for change.

It is written to affirm my two beliefs, "My location doesn't impede my impact." and "My resources are your resources". To acknowledge all the Urban Farmers of Newark, NJ and The Founders of Nonprofit Organizations like Tobias A. Fox and so many others I know whose sacrifice has been the essence of community change and empowerment.

One day I sat at my desk typing and my daughter sitting next to me asked "Mommy what do you do?" to which I answered, "I use my talents and credentials to help change the world." To which Mackaiyah said "Like a superhero?"...
"Yes, Mackaiyah "like a superhero!"

Jacqueleen M. Bido, EdD

#Blessed #EducatedLatina #WholeTeamWinning

PART ONE: Grassroots and The Business of Nonprofit Organizations

"If you don't speak it into existence... then who will?"

-Bidoism

CHAPTER ONE: Grassroots Organizations vs Nonprofits Organizations

"A few people of integrity can go a long way."
-Bill Kauth

The Roots of Grassroots

Imagine if every need or concern you saw growing up in your community was addressed before it impacted you directly? The answer to this is the essence of grassroots organizations. Grassroots organizations are addressing needs or concerns within their community, city, state, nation, country, or the world to eradicate or limit their impact on the people they serve now and in the future. The focus of grassroots organizations can vary. Yet, the constant in grassroots organizations are the PEOPLE.

The People who make up grassroots organizations are not called by the formality of the governing body but rather the necessity of accomplishing the impact being identified as a need. The People come together with the resources they have and the knowledge of what they want to change coupled with action. The People know how to ask for the resources they need in order to further support the impact they would like to make. Grassroots is powered by the passion and dedication of individuals. There are times when the cause is so great that an individual or individuals will take that specific cause and have it support a vision they have for an organization.

Is your grassroots cause something that needs a governance structure? Is it sustainable as it is? Is it or has it been impactful? Do you have what you need for it to be sustainable? Depending on how you answered the previous questions may lead you to seek a formal governance structure. This structure for grassroot causes is traditionally the transition into a nonprofit organization. Can you be a grassroots nonprofit organization? Yes, because even in nonprofit it is about the impact and the people.

What is nonprofit?

A nonprofit is a business. This is a truly important concept for you to understand now because as you delve into this world the business aspect is not sustained by passion alone but by the processes you will implement to be successful. Nonprofits form as corporations at the state level through their Secretary of State's Office. You can be a nonprofit without "IRS tax exemption" as long as you do not intend on receiving donations, making a profit, or applying for grants that require the submission of your IRS 501c3 Affirmation Letter. An IRS tax exempt nonprofit organization by definition is,

> a business that has been granted tax-exempt status by the Internal Revenue Service (IRS) because it furthers a social cause and provides a public benefit.

The key phrases in the definition are:
- a business
- Furthers a social cause and provides a public benefit

When you remember these two things you're setting a great foundation for nonprofit compliance.

The Nonprofit vs The IRS 501c3 Nonprofit vs For Profit

The term "nonprofit" leads to a vast misunderstanding of what charitable organizations do and the role they play in our society. It's not about having or not having a profit. What makes an organization a nonprofit has to do with purpose, ownership, and public support. Charitable nonprofits typically have these elements which include a mission that focuses on activities that benefit society and whose goal is not primarily for profit.

Exempt purposes are considered the following:
- charitable, religious, educational, scientific, literary, testing for public safety, fostering national or international amateur sports competition, and preventing cruelty to children or animals.
- Public ownership where no person owns shares of the corporation or interests in its property.
- Income that must never be distributed to any owners but recycled back into the nonprofit corporation's public benefit mission and activities.

In contrast, a for-profit business typically seeks to generate income for its founders and employees. Most 501(c)(3) nonprofits provide a service, but some are foundations that make grants to other nonprofits to help them pursue their mission. Businesses employ paid staff, while nonprofits may have a workforce made up of both paid staff and volunteers. In fact, in many nonprofits, volunteers outnumber paid employees. Nonprofits may be exempt from federal taxes, and donors to charitable nonprofits may be able to deduct their contributions from federal taxes. To survive, nonprofit organizations, just like businesses, must make sure that the organization's revenues exceed its expenses. But, instead of seeking profit for profit's sake, nonprofits pursue public benefit purposes recognized under federal and state law. It belongs to no private person, and no one person controls the organization and because of this her are some points to remember:

- The assets of a nonprofit are irrevocably dedicated to the charitable, educational, literary, scientific, or religious purposes of the organization.

- The cash, equipment, and other property of a nonprofit cannot be given to anyone or used for anyone's private benefit without fair market compensation to the nonprofit organization.

- A nonprofit's property is permanently dedicated to exempt purposes.

- When and if the organization dissolves, any remaining assets after debts and liabilities are satisfied, must go to another nonprofit organization—not to members of the former nonprofit or any other private individual.

- Control of an incorporated nonprofit lies with a governing board of directors or trustees. The responsibility of that board is to see that the organization fulfills its purpose.

- Board members do not act as individuals but must serve as a group.

- No one has permanent tenure on a board, and the board can, if necessary, fire an executive or remove board members. This means that no one, not even the founder of the organization, can control a nonprofit.

- Most nonprofit boards of directors are not compensated, except for expenses such as travel to and from board meetings.

- Nonprofit organizations are accountable to the public and must file annual information returns with the federal and state governments.

- The federal form that nonprofits must submit is IRS Form 990. The nonprofit must report information regarding its finances, including the salaries of the five highest-paid non-officer employees. IRS public disclosure requirements apply to all tax-exempt organizations. That involves making the nonprofit's three most recent Form 990 or 990-PF returns as well as related supporting documents available to the public. Most nonprofits make them available at their headquarters and on their websites.

- The tax forms are also easily obtained through services such as Guidestar. At the state level, nonprofits are usually overseen by the State's Attorney General's Office.

The difference between The EZ-1023 and the 1023 form

Short Form EZ-1023	Long Form 1023
It requires assets less than $250,000, and forecasted revenue less than $50,000 for the current year and the next two. Costs less money to file.	No revenue limits! More expensive to file than than the EZ-1023

Fiscal Sponsorship

Sometimes a grassroots organization or new nonprofit has not obtained their own 501c3. Some organizations may be in a place where they want to do great work in the community but don't want the responsibility of forming a nonprofit organization. This is where Fiscal Sponsorship can be an avenue to receiving the necessary programmatic funding to carry out the intended program/initiative and overall organizational mission. A fiscal sponsor is,

> a nonprofit organization with an IRS 501c3 that provides fiduciary oversight, financial management, and other administrative services to help build the capacity of charitable projects.

This can be a win/win for a certain organization as you can gain funding for both the organization being sponsored as well as the organization that is the fiscal sponsor which can receive a percentage of the grant awarded. A nonprofit organization with IRS 501c3 exemption can register to be listed on directories as well that are accessible to organizations nationally and globally. The National Council of Nonprofits is an excellent resource of information and in the following infographic they do an excellent job of identifying the roles of Fiscal Sponsor and Sponsored Project.

Roles and responsibilities should be negotiated and documented in a written agreement. Every sponsorship is different, but these are the basics:

Fiscal Sponsorship: Who Does What?

SPONSOR

Lends credibility of 501(c)(3) status to project

Receives and acknowledges charitable contributions

Retains control and discretion over funds

Requests records and reports to fulfill oversight responsibilities

Communicates regularly with project

PROJECT

Has an obligation to disclose to donors that it does not have tax-exempt status

Builds and maintains relationships with donors

Pays administrative fee to and receives flow-through funds from sponsor

Complies with record keeping and reports requested by sponsor

Communicates regularly with sponsor

As fiscal sponsors, tax-exempt organizations can provide infrastructure and support for a start-up project or new organization, as well as a home for the organization's donations.

National Council of **Nonprofits**

The most important parts of fiscal sponsorship are "Integrity" and the "Sponsorship Agreement".

Fiscal Sponsorship Agreement

Agreements should be as detailed as possible. It is common and acceptable for the fiscal sponsor to charge an administrative fee, which is usually a percentage of all funds held on behalf of the sponsored group. Typically this is 5-10% on average. For example:

> If a fiscal sponsor managed $50,000 for your charitable project and they take 10%, the fiscal sponsor would keep $5k. **ESTABLISH THIS IN WRITING!!!**

There are things that should be specifically written in the agreement as it pertains to the management of funds and how they will be paid out. Here are some examples :

- How will the awarded funds be provided? All up front in one lump sum once the award has been received, a percentage of the award broken into payments throughout the funding period, or reimbursement.
- How will the fund be transferred? via check, wire transfer, or bank transfer for documentation purposes. Donations for a specific project should be tracked and delineated to ensure it is directed to the fiscally sponsored entity and project.
- What are the reporting requirements? It will be important for all parties to understand what deliverables and reporting outcomes are needed to ensure award compliance.
- How will programmatic oversight be conducted? Programmatic oversight needs to be clear so that all parties know who is responsible for the program implementation.
- How will we handle dispute or termination of the agreement? Include disclosure statements that speak to what should happen if there is a dispute or the partnership has to be terminated before the completion of the project.

Though it is our intention to have partnerships that work seamlessly there are times where circumstances lead to the necessity to dissolve the partnership for Fiscal Sponsorship. In the end, there are some grassroot organizations that benefit and prefer having these types of fiscal sponsorship without going through the process of becoming an IRS tax exempt 501c3.

Fiscal Sponsorship Agreement Example

On the following page you will see a snapshot of what to include in your agreement. Remember that any template included in this book can be altered to fit the needs of your specific partnership.

Fiscal Sponsorship Agreement

This is a Fiscal Sponsorship Agreement ("Agreement"), dated as of _____, 20__, between Client, a California nonprofit corporation, and _____, an individual ("Project Director").

Background

A. Client is a [_____] nonprofit that [_____]. In line with that mission, Client through its fiscal sponsorship program provides infrastructure and services to projects that further its charitable goals. The program enables projects to focus on their mission and resource development, not on the back office.

B. Project Director wishes to have a project sponsored by Client. The project ("Project") is described in a proposal that Project Director previously submitted to Client. The Client Board of Directors has determined that fiscal sponsorship of the Project advances Client's charitable goals and has approved Client's entry into this Agreement.

Client and Project Director agree as follows:

1. Documents

1.1 This Agreement
This Agreement covers the terms of the sponsorship. It covers, among other things:

- Basic structure of the relationship, including Client's ownership and control of assets
- Project personnel
- Project fundraising and minimum funds requirement
- Project budgeting and spending
- Fees charged by Client
- External communications
- Project oversight and legal compliance
- Sponsorship termination

1.2 Client Policies and Procedures
Client also maintains policies and procedures relating to employees, budgeting, disbursements, communication, branding, and other matters. The key to making this arrangement work is the Project operating within, and taking full advantage of, Client's infrastructure, way of working, and resources.

2. Basic Structure

2.1 Structure and Ownership
Project is a constituent part of Client. Project is not a separate entity and does not have a separate legal status.

2.2 Charitable Status
Project operates under the umbrella of Client's status as a tax-exempt nonprofit organization under Section 501(c)(3) of the Internal Revenue Code ("Code").

The IRS 501c3 Determination Letter and Form 990

The most utilized and requested documents in grant writing are the IRS 501c3 Determination Letter and Form 990 - Return of Organization Exempt From Income Tax. These two documents should be readily available. Out of all of the grants I have been a part of, submitting these documents were requested 99 percent of the time.

```
INTERNAL REVENUE SERVICE                    DEPARTMENT OF THE TREASURY
P. O. BOX 2508
CINCINNATI, OH  45201


Date: AUG 1 8 2014              Employer Identification Number:
                                  47-1446634
                                DLN:
PAWSITIVITY                       504211022
197 GRIGGS STREET N             Contact Person:
SAINT PAUL, MN  55104             CUSTOMER SERVICE          ID# 31954
                                Contact Telephone Number:
                                  (877) 829-5500
                                Accounting Period Ending:
                                  December 31
                                Public Charity Status:
                                  170(b)(1)(A)(vi)
                                Form 990/990-EZ/990-N Required:
                                  Yes
                                Effective Date of Exemption:
                                  July 28, 2014
                                Contribution Deductibility:
                                  Yes
                                Addendum Applies:
                                  No


Dear Applicant:

We're pleased to tell you we determined you're exempt from federal income tax
under Internal Revenue Code (IRC) Section 501(c)(3). Donors can deduct
contributions they make to you under IRC Section 170. You're also qualified to
receive tax deductible bequests, devises, transfers or gifts under Section
2055, 2106, or 2522. This letter could help resolve questions on your exempt
status. Please keep it for your records.

Organizations exempt under IRC Section 501(c)(3) are further classified as
either public charities or private foundations. We determined you're a public
charity under the IRC Section listed at the top of this letter.

If we indicated at the top of this letter that you're required to file Form
990/990-EZ/990-N, our records show you're required to file an annual
information return (Form 990 or Form 990-EZ) or electronic notice (Form 990-N,
the e-Postcard). If you don't file a required return or notice for three
consecutive years, your exempt status will be automatically revoked.

If we indicated at the top of this letter that an addendum applies, the
enclosed addendum is an integral part of this letter.

For important information about your responsibilities as a tax-exempt
organization, go to www.irs.gov/charities. Enter "4221-PC" in the search bar
to view Publication 4221-PC, Compliance Guide for 501(c)(3) Public Charities,
which describes your recordkeeping, reporting, and disclosure requirements.




                                    Letter 5436
```

Form **990**

Return of Organization Exempt From Income Tax

OMB No. 1545-0047

2020

Under section 501(c), 527, or 4947(a)(1) of the Internal Revenue Code (except private foundations)

▶ Do not enter social security numbers on this form as it may be made public.

▶ Go to www.irs.gov/Form990 for instructions and the latest information.

Open to Public Inspection

Department of the Treasury
Internal Revenue Service

A For the 2020 calendar year, or tax year beginning _____, 2020, and ending _____, 20___

B Check if applicable:	**C** Name of organization	**D** Employer identification number
☐ Address change	Doing business as	
☐ Name change	Number and street (or P.O. box if mail is not delivered to street address) Room/suite	**E** Telephone number
☐ Initial return		
☐ Final return/terminated	City or town, state or province, country, and ZIP or foreign postal code	**G** Gross receipts $
☐ Amended return	**F** Name and address of principal officer:	**H(a)** Is this a group return for subordinates? ☐ Yes ☐ No
☐ Application pending		**H(b)** Are all subordinates included? ☐ Yes ☐ No

I Tax-exempt status: ☐ 501(c)(3) ☐ 501(c)( ) ◀ (insert no.) ☐ 4947(a)(1) or ☐ 527

If "No," attach a list. See instructions

J Website: ▶

H(c) Group exemption number ▶

K Form of organization: ☐ Corporation ☐ Trust ☐ Association ☐ Other ▶   **L** Year of formation: **M** State of legal domicile:

Part I Summary

Activities & Governance

1 Briefly describe the organization's mission or most significant activities: _____

2 Check this box ▶ ☐ if the organization discontinued its operations or disposed of more than 25% of its net assets.

3	Number of voting members of the governing body (Part VI, line 1a)	**3**	
4	Number of independent voting members of the governing body (Part VI, line 1b)	**4**	
5	Total number of individuals employed in calendar year 2020 (Part V, line 2a)	**5**	
6	Total number of volunteers (estimate if necessary)	**6**	
7a	Total unrelated business revenue from Part VIII, column (C), line 12	**7a**	
b	Net unrelated business taxable income from Form 990-T, Part I, line 11	**7b**	

		Prior Year	Current Year
Revenue	8 Contributions and grants (Part VIII, line 1h)		
	9 Program service revenue (Part VIII, line 2g)		
	10 Investment income (Part VIII, column (A), lines 3, 4, and 7d)		
	11 Other revenue (Part VIII, column (A), lines 5, 6d, 8c, 9c, 10c, and 11e)		
	12 Total revenue—add lines 8 through 11 (must equal Part VIII, column (A), line 12)		
Expenses	13 Grants and similar amounts paid (Part IX, column (A), lines 1–3)		
	14 Benefits paid to or for members (Part IX, column (A), line 4)		
	15 Salaries, other compensation, employee benefits (Part IX, column (A), lines 5–10)		
	16a Professional fundraising fees (Part IX, column (A), line 11e)		
	b Total fundraising expenses (Part IX, column (D), line 25) ▶		
	17 Other expenses (Part IX, column (A), lines 11a–11d, 11f–24e)		
	18 Total expenses. Add lines 13–17 (must equal Part IX, column (A), line 25)		
	19 Revenue less expenses. Subtract line 18 from line 12		

		Beginning of Current Year	End of Year
Net Assets or Fund Balances	20 Total assets (Part X, line 16)		
	21 Total liabilities (Part X, line 26)		
	22 Net assets or fund balances. Subtract line 21 from line 20		

Part II Signature Block

Under penalties of perjury, I declare that I have examined this return, including accompanying schedules and statements, and to the best of my knowledge and belief, it is true, correct, and complete. Declaration of preparer (other than officer) is based on all information of which preparer has any knowledge.

Sign Here	▶ Signature of officer	Date
	▶ Type or print name and title	

Paid Preparer Use Only	Print/Type preparer's name	Preparer's signature	Date	Check ☐ if self-employed	PTIN
	Firm's name ▶			Firm's EIN ▶	
	Firm's address ▶			Phone no.	

May the IRS discuss this return with the preparer shown above? See instructions   ☐ Yes ☐ No

For Paperwork Reduction Act Notice, see the separate instructions.   Cat. No. 11282Y   Form **990** (2020)

The Work

Nonprofit Leader

1. Do you want a nonprofit organization?
2. Why do you want a nonprofit organization?
3. Do you need your own tax-exemption to do what you need to do? or Do you need a fiscal sponsor to do what you need to do?
4. Have you ever thought about being a fiscal sponsor for an organization?
5. Are you registered on Guidestar? https://www.guidestar.org/search
6. Do you need a fiscal sponsor for your organization as you await your 501c3 Determination?

Grant Writer

1. What do you understand about the functions of a nonprofit organization?
2. What is the difference to you between a fiscally sponsored organization and an independently tax-exempt 501c3 nonprofit organization?
3. What kind of nonprofit do you want to write for?
    a. Is it large, small, or both?
    b. Are you a staff member or independent contractor affiliated with the nonprofit?
4. How much time are you willing to dedicate to the nonprofit grant writing process?

Call to Action

Reflect on the community you are in. Think about a time growing up where you wish there was an organization that had a resource you needed to help you or provide something for you. What was it that you needed? Was there an organization to fulfill it? If yes, reach out to that organization and tell them the impact they had in your life. If no, reach out to an organization that is fulfilling this need in the community and tell them how important they are to the community.

CHAPTER TWO: The Power of Preparation

"Give me six hours to chop down a tree and I will spend

the first four sharpening the axe." -

-Abraham Lincoln

Preparation and You

The power of preparation is driven by the process you implement. The final proposal is only the end result of the process you implemented prior to its development and completion. Now let's see how much time you spend in each of the following categories …

How much time do you spend in hours on the following tasks?

1. Sharing your mission in any way
2. Researching Grant opportunities
3. Networking at different events to gain partnerships
4. Networking at different events to gain funding or funding resources
5. Professionally developing yourself and staff in the the area of your mission
6. Reviewing programmatic data to assess your impact and success
7. Forecasting your work ahead of time
8. Identifying your staffing needs and sustainability

The previous list is a snapshot of some of the most important things you should have a process for as throughout this book you will see how it all is integrated in not just submitting a successful grant proposal but a successful nonprofit organization.

Understanding your Mission

"Without a mission statement, you may get to the top of the ladder and then

realise it was leaning against the wrong building."

Dave Ramsey

Two very important questions about yourself about the mission:

What are you impacting?

and

Why are you impacting it?

Why is it important for grant writing? These are integral aspects to understand when you are applying for grants. Understanding the "WHY?" is essential in directing your next steps in program development and seeking the funding you need to sustain it. It also informs you on several other factors such as partnerships, potential funders, and the data necessary to prove you are doing what you say you're doing.

Mission Statement Examples

Newark Science and Sustainability, Inc. (Newark SAS)

Sustainability, Inc. (Newark SaS) is a community-driven, 501c3 nonprofit organization based in Newark, NJ that creates generational sustainability through the implementation of educational programs, agricultural training, and community green development initiatives to ensure eco-conscious communities and healthy food access locally and globally.

'

Urban Agriculture Cooperative (UAC)

Our mission is to enhance a localized food system for historically underserved growers and consumers lacking healthy food access.

Al-Munir LLC

Al-Munir LLC is a multidisciplinary consulting firm founded in 2016 that offers opportunities to impact policy-change through community organizing, focus groups, and arts and culture.

Elevate Newark

Elevate Newark was established on April 14th, 2020 with a mission to impact and empower individuals, businesses, and nonprofit organizations throughout the City of Newark.

The previous examples are just a few mission statements for you to begin to see how they vary from entity to entity. As you begin to look at the organization's mission whether creating a mission statement for your own organization or reviewing them as a grant writer it is important to note the focus of the mission. Funders will look at your mission statement to assess at time the alignment of your mission with the funding area of focus. This allows for organizations who truly impact a specific arena to receive funding because it is true to their mission or level of expertise. While this doesn't restrict you from applying for all kinds of funding it is important to be able to show the experience one has in addressing the intended funding focus. Your mission in the end is a driving force for your programmatic next steps.

The Work

Nonprofit Leader

Do you have a mission? If yes, go to question number 3. If no take a moment to reflect on a need or the needs in your community:

    a. write down everything you see as a need.

    b. Now place a star next to the needs you feel you can have a positive impact on.

    c. Prioritize those needs from highest amount of impact to minimal amount of impact.

    d. Write your name next to the needs you want to address.

What is your mission?

Have you ever been impacted by the need your mission is addressing?

Why is this your mission?

The Grant Writer

1. What do you understand about the organization's mission you are writing for?

2. Why is this their mission?

3. What programming would an organization with a mission like this do?

Call to Action

Look up the mission statement of a large and small nonprofit organization that you know of. Take their mission and highlight the work you feel they are doing that aligns to their mission on your social media or with another person.

CHAPTER THREE: Signature Programs, Products and Services

When you learn, teach. When you get, give."
– Maya Angelou

As a nonprofit evolves it is necessary that programming continue to evolve as well. There are times that will call for innovative projects that highlight the expertise of the organization and increase the impact on the community. In other occasions the needs of the community will call for programming to be focused and consistent. This is done through what I call "Signature Programming".

Signature Programs

Every nonprofit should have signature programs and initiatives that the community can count on. Establishing signature programs in alignment with your mission enables the ability to:

- Helps build your organizational brand
- Increases your ability to gain valuable data
- It helps builds relationships with your key stakeholders

For 12 years Newark Science and Sustainability, Inc., has been hosting the Sustainable Living Empowerment Conference.

The Necessity of Consistency

When it comes to sustaining a nonprofit organization, consistency will build the trust of the people. Quite often there are nonprofits that exist "in name only". When community stakeholders are asked what do they do? or when it comes time to cite their impact there is nothing to assess. Now one can assume it is because of a lack of money yet when you are a new nonprofit there are things you can still do as you are pooling your resources. If you are a new nonprofit with limited resources what you can provide is knowledge and access to resources that come from existing entities while you are building your own organizational capacity. There is always something you can do to show that you are in alignment with the definition of a nonprofit of "providing a benefit to the community". Take for instance Newark Science and Sustainability, Inc. we have provided countless hours of training and access to resources even before we had a budget that could sustain it. Oftentimes providing and garnering services as in-kind donations as no cost to the stakeholder. When you prioritize the people in your community you will find a way that limits the impact on the stakeholders especially when we are serving community members living below the national poverty level.

It is imperative that you are able to market your offerings both at your location and the many social media platforms available to do so. There are platforms that will allow you to create an event, register participants virtually, and track the data. This is important to do especially with grant writing as it will provide the necessary data funders look for when deciding what programs to fund. An example of this is Eventbrite which allows you the ability to do what was described previously. Here is an example:

Newark Science and Sustainability, Inc.

Follow

Events   Collections New

Free   Free   Free

Feeding the Soil
Thu, May 11, 4:00 PM
438 Peshine Ave • Newark, NJ
Free

Farm to Kitchen, Cooking for Busy People
Fri, Apr 21, 1:00 PM
36 Rose Terrace • Newark, NJ
Free

Indoor Farming through Hydroponics, a solution based practice
Sat, Apr 15, 11:00 AM
Newark Beth Israel Medical Cent...
Free

Urban Agriculture as a Catalyst for Community Development
Wed, Mar 29, 2023 6:30 PM EDT
Free

Can a Nonprofit Sell Goods and Services?

So, can nonprofits sell goods and services? Yes, you can! Though nonprofits cannot make a profit, you still need to make income in order to support your cause. Merchandise, goods, and services are great ways for a nonprofit to increase revenue. Therefore, nonprofits can sell goods and services as long as you use the money to fund your programs without providing any profit to stakeholders.

Product vs Services

A product is a tangible item that is put on the market for acquisition, attention, or consumption, while a service is an intangible item, which arises from the output of one or more individuals. Although it seems like the main distinction between the two concepts is founded on their tangibility, that is not always the case. In most cases services are intangible, but products are not always tangible. The following activity will assist you in brainstorming this definition:

The Mint Org.

The following exercise will help you identify potential products and services for your own organization.

Scenario:

The Mint Co. is attempting to increase their products and services. The mission of this organization is to produce the best organic mint to increase the health of the community

Directions:

You have two minutes to write all of the possible products and services for the Mint. Co.

Products:

What are the possible products of the Mint Leaf Company?

Services:

What are the possible services of the Mint Leaf Company?

Do any of the products and services that include art?

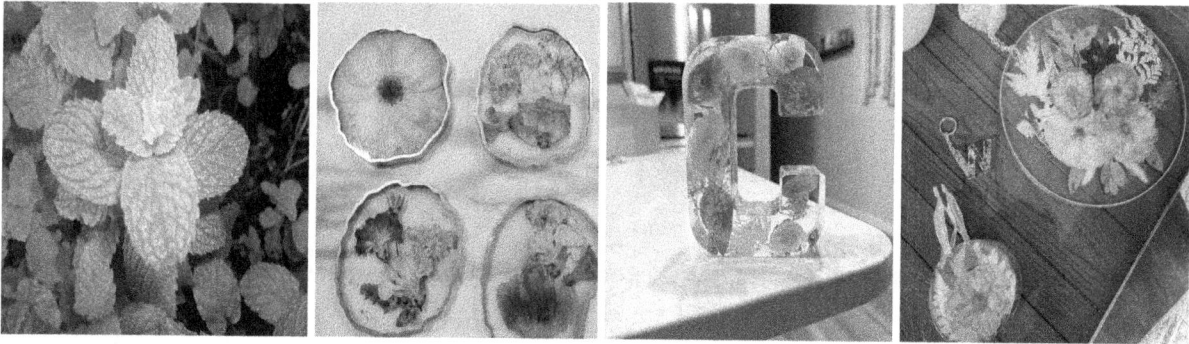

The aforementioned is a very important exercise to do as too often nonprofit entities do not identify their own products and services. As a leader there is expertise that you and other members of the organization can speak to as subject matter experts. You can be contracted by for-profit companies or other entities to bring that expertise into their network. By establishing products and services like the example provided you are able to increase the name recognition of your organization as well as potential resources and volunteers. The more people from your organization can get in front of the people to share your mission, your impact, and the many ways they can support your mission the more your organization will grow.

Restrictions on Selling Services and Merchandise

There are a few restrictions that nonprofits need to be aware of when selling goods and services, especially concerning nonprofit revenue. First, as we mentioned before, the goods or services must be related to the mission of the nonprofit. Additionally, nonprofits can only sell goods or services at reasonable prices. You cannot charge an excessive amount just because you have a nonprofit. In addition, your nonprofit cannot use your goods or services to unfairly compete with for-profit businesses. Lastly, any revenue generated from selling goods and services must go back to your nonprofit to support your programs – it cannot be distributed among stakeholders. Here are some additional example:

T-shirts: T-shirts are always a popular item, especially if they have a catchy phrase or design. Nonprofits can sell t-shirts to both supporters and the general public.

Coffee or Tea Mugs: Like t-shirts, coffee mugs are popular and can be sold to supporters and the general public.

Programs: If a nonprofit offers programs, they can charge a fee for these programs. For example, if a nonprofit has an after-school program, they can charge parents a per-day or monthly fee.

Training: Nonprofits can also sell training sessions. This could be anything from cooking classes to financial literacy courses.

Consulting: Nonprofits can provide consulting services to other nonprofits or businesses. This can be a great way to generate revenue while also helping others.

Events: Nonprofits can also charge for tickets to events that they host. For example, if a nonprofit hosts a gala, they can sell tickets to the event.

As a grant writer it will be necessary to understand your organization's programs, products and services because these will be the foundation of your grant proposal. These things can be written into a grant proposal so that it may be funded. In addition, a great grant writer knows how to develop or research comparable programs that will increase the impact of the organization as well as the likelihood of being funded. It will be best practice to engage in conferences where there are many stakeholders from the nonprofit sector to learn more about what is happening in the arenas. These conferences can be local, national and even global which will expose you to the need and how it is being addressed in different areas.

The Work
Nonprofit Leader
1. How many products did you come up with for the Mint Co.?
2. How many services did you come up with for the Mint Co.?
3. What programs, products, and services does your organization offer?
4. Independently and then with a group of people conduct the following:
    a. Enter Your Organization Name
    b. Enter Your Mission
    c. Set a timer for Two Minutes.
    d. Independently or with your board, focus group, community members, and or youth.
    e. Provide the following directions: You have two minutes to write all of the possible products and services for (Enter your organization's name).
        i. Products: What are the possible products of (Enter Organization Name)?

      ii.   Services: What are the possible services of (Enter Organization Name)?

   f. Now collect all of the answers and track them on a singular sheet. Discuss the answers provided.

   g. Put a star on all products and services that are not currently active or available.

   h. Have the group explain how they feel about what they see? If independently done, reflect on what you see?

   i. What is the intended outcome of these programs, products, and services?

5. Have you attended any conferences this year?

6. What local, national, or global conferences will you be attending this year?

7. Make a list of potential conferences you can present at and select three to submit a proposal to.

Grant Writer

1. What programs, products, and services does the organization you write for offer?

2. Why have they selected these programs, products, and services?

3. What is the intended outcome of these programs, products, and services?

4. What additional programs, products, and services would you suggest they provide to increase funding streams and above all impact?

5. What local, national, or global conferences will you be attending this year?

Call to Action

Identify a nonprofit organization. This can be your own or another. Select a program they are currently offering or a service they are offering that you feel is successful. Share a post about the product or service.

CHAPTER FOUR: Research

"Research is seeing what everybody else has seen and
thinking what nobody else has thought."
- Albert Szent-Györgyi

Research By Definition

Research by definition is the systematic investigation into and study of materials and sources in order to establish facts and reach new or validate existing conclusions. Research is imperative not only for your mission but also for grant writing purposes. Many grant reviewers will want and Request For Proposals (RFP) will request you to support your opinion by citing research. Research can and should be cited locally, regionally, nationally, and globally depending on the area your organization is impacting or intends to impact in the future.

Accessing Research

You can access the research conducted by other individuals to support the validity of your mission. The following will identify just a few of the many resources you can utilize:

Civil Rights Data US Department of Education

For more than five decades, the Civil Rights Data Collection has captured data on students' equal access to educational opportunities to understand and inform schools' compliance with the civil rights laws enforced by the Department of Education's Office for Civil Rights. https://civilrightsdata.ed.gov/

Agriculture

The Economic Research Service USDA offers an array of information, publications as well as visual maps and research under topics section.

USDA

The US Department of Agriculture offers access to an array of resources and their current priorities are:

- Advancing Racial Justice, Equity, and Opportunity
- Addressing Climate Change
- Tackling Food and Nutrition Insecurity
- More, Better, and New Market Opportunities

Google Scholar

Google Scholar provides a simple way to broadly search for scholarly literature.

Universities

Seton Hall's eRepository is an online institutional repository and archive that collects, preserves, and distributes digital materials produced by members of the Seton Hall community for use by the university community and beyond.

State, County, or City Master Plans

Newark360m Master Plan

The City of Newark New Jersey engaged stakeholders on every level in or to develop the city's master plan. This plan outlines the goals and needs of the city and the areas they seek to address. We use this document to see what our organizations can do to support the city's plan.

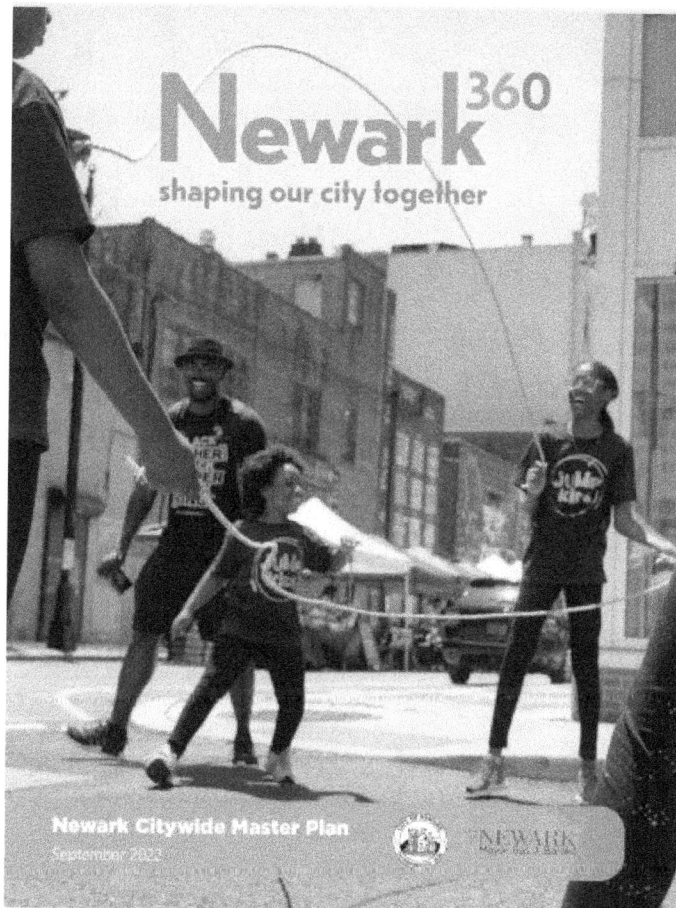

Goal 4: Leverage sustainable development to improve outdoor air quality.

Actions	Plan Element	Timeframe (S - 1 year, M 2-5 years, L - 10 years)	Department Responsible
4.4.1 Develop and support a citywide tree canopy initiative.	Sustainability	Medium	Sustainability
4.4.2 Create landscape buffers to protect communities from highways and sources of pollution.	Sustainability	Medium	Engineering, Sustainability
4.4.3 Identify and mitigate point source pollution from heavy industry and energy infrastructure.	Sustainability	Medium	Engineering, Sustainability

Goal 5: Expand access to resources for healthier living.

Actions	Plan Element	Timeframe (S - 1 year, M 2-5 years, L - 10 years)	Department Responsible
4.5.1 Designate and support urban agriculture zones within each Ward	Sustainability	Medium	EHD, Sustainability
4.5.2 Create and incentivize neighborhood based fresh food access/grocery stores.	Sustainability	Medium	EHD
4.5.3 Create and incentivize neighborhood based health clinics.		Medium	

Local and Global Strategic Plans

The Division for Sustainable Development Goals (DSDG) in the United Nations Department of Economic and Social Affairs (UNDESA) acts as the Secretariat for the SDGs, providing substantive support and capacity-building for the goals and their related thematic issues, including water, energy, climate, oceans, urbanization, transport, science and technology, the Global Sustainable Development Report (GSDR), partnerships and Small Island Developing States.

The Work

Nonprofit Leader

1. What does research say about your community, its stakeholders, its needs, its issues, etc.

2. Does your city, state, or county have a master plan?

3. What goals within the master plan align to your current mission or organizational goals?

4. Are their countries addressing the concerns of your mission?

5. Utilize the template to begin identifying your organization alignment in each category independently or with your team.

Grant Writer

1. Reflect on the mission of the organization you are writing for. What research exist to justify the need and or the program, products, or services being implemented?/

2. What is does research say about the community from the following lenses:

    a. Health

    b. Climate

    c. Violence

    d. The Arts

      e. Education

      f. Economy

      g. Equity

      h. Housing

      i. Poverty

      j. Politics

      k. Other (enter your own topic)

3. Create a folder on your computer, Google Drive, or other platform and for each category mentioned in question 2 create a sub-folder. Search for research for each category. As you come across a resource or document in alignment with the topic, download it and save it in its specific folder. This will enable you quick access to research to reference in grant writing now and later.

Call to Action

Identify a resource that highlights research that you feel the local community should know. If it is aligned with your organization's mission, pogroms, products, or services make sure you mention it. For example, research that speaks to food deserts should include a statement that says "while this research notes food deserts in our community our mission is to address them by (insert your example). Then continue to speak about your organization or link the reader to your website.

CHAPTER FIVE: Data Collection

"In God we trust. All others must bring data."
-W. Edwards Deming

What is Data?

Data is facts and statistics collected together for reference or analysis.

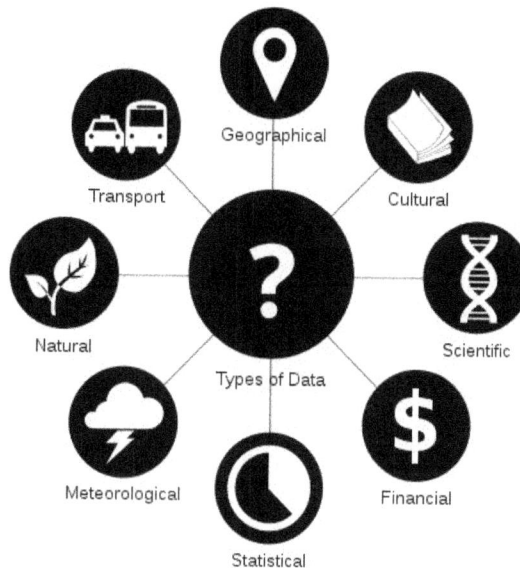

Data is all around us and when it comes to writing grants data is an important aspect of the proposal especially when you are speaking about community needs, demographics, organizational impact, etc. As a nonprofit leader data should be collected and analyzed in order to understand your own impact as well as drive the direction of the organization.

Top Six Data Collection Methods

1. **Interviews -** An interview is a qualitative research method that relies on asking questions in order to collect data. Interviews involve two or more people, one of whom is the interviewer asking the questions.

2. **Questionnalres and surveys -** A questionnaire is a research instrument consisting of a series of questions designed to collect data from respondents.

3. **Observations -** are a method of collecting and recording data by observing and noting events, behaviors, or phenomena in a systematic and objective manner

4. **Documents and records -**Documents and records are a data collection method that involves collecting data from existing sources such as reports, historical records, and

official documents.

5. **Focus groups** - A focus group is a research method that brings together a small group of people to answer questions in a moderated setting. The group is chosen due to predefined demographic traits, and the questions are designed to shed light on a topic of interest.

6. **Oral histories** - Oral history is a method of conducting historical research through recorded interviews between a narrator with personal experience of historically significant events and a well-informed interviewer, with the goal of adding to the historical record.

Of the data collection methods mentioned above, how many have you utilized in your own organization?

Data Collection Life Cycle

Twilio Segment identified 8 points in the Data Collection Life Cycle:

- Generation
- Collection
- Processing
- Storage
- Management
- Analysis
- Visualization
- Interpretation

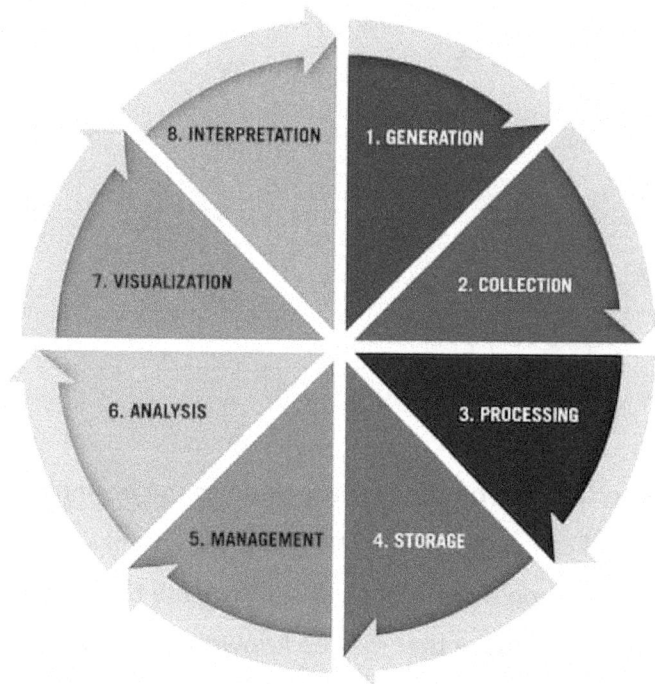

Data collection is important but more important than the collection are the questions we ask and the analysis of the answers given.

Write one or two words to describe what you have gotten from this read thus far.

_____

_____

Imagine if you post this question at every event, the words can be combined in a word cloud, create themes for outcomes, or provide a perspective to either keep or evolve your training.

The Learning Scale

For years in my time in academia it was commonplace to establish a learning scale when conducting a training or professional development. The Learning Scale allowed me the opportunity collect data pre, during, and post training session just by asking a single question:

Tell me where you are on the Learning Scale?

4	I am a grant writer who has won more than one grant and can support others in doing the same.
3	I know the fundamental of grant writing, have written a grant, and can teach them to others.
2	I know the fundamentals of grant writing and can write a grant.
1	I know some of the fundamentals of grant writing but have not written a grant.
0	I have never written a grant and do not know the fundamentals of grant writing.

By asking the group where they are on the learning scale at the beginning via sticky note, a show of hands, or in a chat I can assess immediately if the room has novice knowledge or mastery. This knowledge helps me make real-time adjustments to the pacing of the lesson and the integration of defining terminology that may be known to the stakeholders in the room. In a room of mastery I integrate more conversation about strategy and process as we go through the presentation. You may ask yourself, "what data can you glean just from that question?" Well,

- depending on the number lets say it was 20 people and 10 said they were on scale level 0. I can say, 50 percent of the attendees came in at a novice level as it pertained to (insert training topic).
- During the training I can see and assess learning gains by how the attendees answer the question and can say "25 percent of those who said they were novice learners increase knowledge by the midpoint of the training"

and so forth.

If this training is given multiple times a year then you can take all of the data and state things like,

- 75 percent of participants (100 participants) came in at a novice scale level. This data supports the need for additional training to increase the knowledge of attendees who come from (enter location, income level, demographics, gender, age, etc.).

The Levels of Understanding

You can have multiple levels of understanding depending on the progression of the intended outcome. Traditionally, there are 5 levels of understanding 1-5. In my version I include Level 0 as in the years of community engagement and training I have had participants who have never heard of the topic until entering the room. This was especially prevalent with topics addressing Climate Justice and Community Violence Intervention. The following is an example of the levels interpretation that can be modified to fit the specific training like the one shared earlier.

Training Topic/Goal	
Level 5	I am very confident or experienced. I can teach someone how to do this.
Level 4	I can do this on my own. I can show I understand.
Level 3	I can or have done this with help or with an example in front of me.
Level 2	I have some understanding. I know some of the terminology used in this topic.
Level 1	I have some understanding but have little knowledge of terminology.
Level 0	I have never heard of this topic and or have no understanding or knowledge of topic terminology.

The point of the aforementioned example is to show how you can collect data to justify the importance of a program, product, service, etc. through real time data collection. This method also allows for the trainer to assess if the training outcome is actually being met. When it is not one can make the necessary adjustment to do so.

When it comes to data it is important to have a process in place for data collection management that aligns to the Data Collection Life Cycle. This is necessary because in at least 95 percent of grant applications there are questions that will explicitly ask you about how data is collected and managed. Do you currently have the information needed to answer all of the following questions?

Describe your organization's experience and capacity to collect and manage data, including confidential data **(15 points).**

1. What demographic data does your organization collect and how often is it collected?

2. Describe the systems and/or databases your organization uses to collect data for each of the activities. How will you collect, maintain, and report data for each

activity?

Defining Impact

There are two interpretations of the definition of impact:

1. come into forcible contact with another object.
2. have a strong effect on someone or something.

In definition number one imagine a car accident making an impact. You can see it, hear it, and feel it. In definition number two imagine your organization's mission, program, products, services, initiatives, etc. and ask yourself this:

1. How will your impact be seen?

- Data Presentation
- Documentaries
- Photography
- Social Media Posts
- Webinars
- Programming
- Events
- Open House

2. How will your impact be heard?

- Workshops
- Podcasts
- Webinars
- Word of Mouth
- Open House

3. How will your impact be felt?

By:

- The members of the organization
- The participants
- The community

The Work

Nonprofit Leader

1. Complete the following Learning Scale with your own topic and outcomes independently or with your team.

LEARNING SCALE	
Training Topic/Goal	
Level 5	
Level 4	
Level 3	
Level 2	
Level 1	
Level 0	

2. What data collection methods have you used?
3. What new data collection methods will you integrate into your process?
4. Do you have a Data Collection Lifecycle plan?
5. How will you utilize the Data Collection Lifecycle in your organization?
6. How will your impact be seen?
7. How will your impact be heard?
8. How will your impact be felt?
9. What does your current data say about your organization?
10. What additional data do you need to collect that you aren't currently tracking?

Grant Writer

1. Identify how data is collected in the organization you are writing for?
2. Align data collected by the organization to the respective program or initiative.
3. How did you first find out about this organization's impact?
4. What strategy for impact can the organization you write for add to increase their reach?

Call to Action

For the/your organization create a data post sharing the impact your or an organization has had attending a specific program. For examples of this go to www.sasglocal.com .

CHAPTER SIX: Partnering Organizations

"In the midst of chaos, there is also opportunity"
– Sun Tzu

To Partner or Not to Partner

RFP's consistently ask about who you are partnering with. One reason for this question is that funders want to see that you are collaborating with other key stakeholders within your community. It allows for funding to benefit the community in ways that your mission alone cannot reach but collectively can change an entire community. In order to build a network of partnering organizations the following template was created. This template allows for the identification of organizations, their expertise, and the alignment to specific areas of focus. When you begin filling in this information you are able to engage these entities specifically and explicitly. As funding opportunities are released and require collaboration this document will assist in facilitating the entities you want to include. This document should be updated at minimum quarterly. To put this into practice, set a calendar invitation to research other entities, schedule introductory meetings with leadership, align programmatic offerings and if available include any forecasted costs.

Identifying Partner Alignment

NCFS Organization Focus Programs and Expertise

Food Access	Organization Name	Program/Initiative/Activity Name, short description
	Urban Agriculture Cooperative (UAC)	The Cooperative Market emphasizes food sovereignty and empowerment in agriculture by prioritizing products supplied by Newark based food producers, with an emphasis on small lot urban growers, BIPOC and women-owned farm businesses, and family farms with demonstrated commitment to urban food access for our City of Newark and the greater region.

There are over 1.5 million nonprofit organizations in the United States. There are plenty of entities to collaborate with. One thing to keep in mind in all partnerships **"PUT EVERYTHING IN WRITING!!!!"** Understand the importance of clear communication channels and transparency if there are any issues or concerns throughout the grant funding period. This is especially important in federally funded grants where an entity takes the role as lead applicant. A Partnership Agreement or Memorandum of Understanding is often a requirement for grant submission or at the time the funding has been awarded. In addition, in a recent Environmental Protection Agency Notice of Funding (aka RFP) it was required that in the agreement the process for transitioning a partnering organization be included in the agreement in writing.

How Many Is Too Many?

When it comes to partnering there isn't really a "Too Many" as long as you have clear communication and processes in place for navigating the many moving parts. In times where you have multiple partners it is important to establish reporting metrics ahead of time especially for federally funded grants as compliance for these types of grants is very specific. You never want to put yourself in a situation where you don't have the answers you need because a consistent porting process was not in place. We will go into this in more detail later on in this book. Again, it is necessary to have a clear **Process, Process, Process.**

The Work

Nonprofit Leader

1. Make a list of organizations in your local community, city, county, state, nationally, and globally that you would like to collaborate with. Prioritize the organizations you know have initiatives that align to your mission.

2. Create a list of themes/categories your organization focuses on.

3. Complete the Partner Alignment template. Go to www.bidoism.com to download the template.

Grant Writer

1. Identify the areas of focus the nonprofit you write for is focused on.

2. Create or obtain a Partner Alignment template.

3. Have or create an accessible list for the organizations that exist locally in the community in order to build a database of potential partners to recommend to an organization.

Call To Action

1. Identify an organization in your community.

2. Create a post, text, or email describing the impact you have seen, heard, or felt.

3. Tag me on LinkedIn and I will reshare it.

CHAPTER SEVEN: Summary

"Genius is in the idea. Impact, however, comes from action."

-Simon Sinek

Nonprofit Leader

Dear Nonprofit Leader,

Throughout Part One you have been posed several questions that will and or could help you reflect on where you are or where you want to go when it comes to the formation of a nonprofit organization. It was the intention of part one for you to look at your current or future programming products and services with fresh eyes. The understanding of impact as it relates to data collection and research. As you progress to Part Two we will engage you in topics that prepare you to have an honest conversation about money, resources and the accountability that comes with it in the world of nonprofit organizations. It is important in the next chapter that no matter what your funding status is, that you do not lose hope or passion for the work you have been called to do that transcends money. Stay steadfast in doing the work of the people.

Grant Writer

Dear Grant Writer,

Throughout Part One many of your tasks and call to action were geared toward sharing information about a specific organization, data, etc. This was by intention because grant writing takes understanding the pulse of the community being served. It is important that you begin to build a profile and network of organizations that can be called upon to bring a grant proposal to fruition. Initially you may feel as if you are overwhelmed by what to include or not to include. These feelings are natural and you will overcome them the more you know the organization you write for. There are times where the data does not exist and you will have to utilize what you have qualitatively to articulate impact within a program or proposal. I will say that throughout my career I do not write for just anyone. The organizations I have written for must do the work of the people. I pride myself in using these gifts to impact community change. This has made all the difference for me and my writing. It may not be the same for you and that is okay. As you engage in Part Two you will begin to understand the necessity for cohesiveness from mission, to program, to the budget, and to the intended impact. Even if you are not a numbers person you must become one in grant writing. It is imperative that you understand

59

how to disaggregate the funding amount in a way that makes sense as the budget narrative will ensure that it does. No pressure... just awareness that will make you a better grant writer as you take on more and more grants.

PART TWO: Money Matters

"How you handle a single dollar is how you will handle one million"
- Bidoism

CHAPTER EIGHT: The Cost of Impact

"Many people take no care of their money till they come nearly to the end of it,
and others do just the same with their time."
- Johann Wolfgang von Goethe

What Does It Cost?

Understanding the cost of your program and its alignment to your mission and the needs of the community will assist you in applying for funding. For each program you need to create the follow:

Program/Initiative	Overview	Outcome	Cost	Data Collected
Annual Sustainability Conference	An annual conference that engages key stakeholders in presentations that will empower them to take action in their local community.	Increased environmental awareness Increased implementation of environmentally friendly practices	$5000	Surveys Interview Focus Group Visual Artifacts

As well as an individual program budget that delineates everything it takes to bring that initiative to fruition. What I have seen is that in grassroots is that everything is grouped together on one organizational budget. This is okay to depict the overall organizational budget but makes it difficult to decipher what programs are truly costly to implement. Whether it is a one off program or initiative a budget breakdown should exist. By creating these separate budget breakdowns you will be able to look at real-time staffing needs, supply needs, transportation needs, participant numbers, and then compare the cost to the intended impact. When looking at your programs one should attempt to drill down to the cost per participant. For instance:

If the total all in cost of your program is $10,000 and you have 20 participants then the total cost per participant is $500.

The aforementioned example helps you with programmatic fundraising because you can personify the direct impact of the donation to a participant. For example:

For a donation of $500 dollars you can sponsor one participant in enrolling in a coding program. Upon completion the participant will be certified in entry level coding."

Or

"With a donation of $10,000 dollars you can sponsor 20 youth in learning how to grow their own food using hydroponics."

The Needs List

There is something that is integral for organizations to integrate into their organization and that is the sharing of a "Needs List". A needs list is exactly how it sounds: a list of your organization's needs. When you create your needs lists you can put anything you want on it. You can delineate even volunteer services. You can have on the list some of the following example:

- 1 green house 40x40 = $40,000
- 45 boxes of crayons 48 count = $225
- 20 hrs of bookkeeping services = $5000
- 4 hours of volunteer harvesting of leafy greens = $200
- 10 bookbags = $250
- An electric van = $50,000
- Outdoor Refrigerator = $9,000
- 10 Interns for 6 months for 20 hours a month = $50,000
- 15 Chickens = $2000
- A Tool Shed = $5,000
- $25 Dollar Gift Cards = Unlimited
- Other - Please contact to donate something not on the list.

This list can include everything you consider a need. When you take the time to identify everything you need these needs can be fulfilled by individual donors or groups of donors. There is something I learned about donors which I consistently keep in mind when I am working with various organizations and that is that Donors fall into the following categories:

Goods - anything on the list that are tangibles and can be purchased

Money - monetary donations in gift cards, currency, and or through their Will.

Time - the donation of time providing subject matter expertise in a given arena and or physical labor.

I like to include the monetary equivalent with the needs list and as many details as possible. While we could assume that receiving a monetary donation is the priority, many donors I have come across like to know specifically how their donation is being used. There are times where families have come together to donate to a specific organization.

This needs list should then be turned into a pdf, or another visual medium to be shared on social media. The needs list can be added to your website or linked to your social media pages. There should be specific contact information included in the document or the visual medium utilized for sharing. As a rule of thumb ensure that whatever contact information is utilized that it is a contact that is active and accessible. This ensures that when people are ready to donate from your needs list they can.

The Work

Nonprofit Leader

1. Complete individually or with your team the Cost of Impact Program Alignment Template. Be sure to include both active and anticipated programs/initiatives.
2. Create a needs list for your organization. Be as comprehensive as possible.
3. Create a pdf and or visual of this needs list.

Grant Writer

1. Assist an organization in completing the Cost of Impact Program Alignment Template. If you are completing this with an organization you write to keep a copy of this completed template. It will assist you as you come across various grants that may be in alignment with the organization.
2. Assist and organization in the creation of a needs list. Keep a copy of the list and brainstorm possible justification for each item. This practice will help you when addressing the Budget Narrative depending on what items may be included in your proposal budget as allowable costs.

Call To Action

Obtain a needs list and share it on your social media platform. Pick an item off of the needs list and make an individual donation of goods, money or time.

CHAPTER NINE: The Master Budget, The Program Budget, The Grant Budget and The Reality

"A budget is telling your money where to go instead of wondering where it went."

– John Maxwell

The Reality

So I will hit you with the reality first, out of all of the topics in this book the budget in and of itself has caused the most anxiety in grant writing and or nonprofit governance. This anxiety is meritted due to the fact that the budget tells a story about your organization's needs and nonprofit fiscal standings. It can tell a funder immediately in some instances where you are, plan and need to go financially. Within the various versions and methods to track or depict where money is and needs to be, the budget is very important. How you direct the funds in different categories also speaks volumes. If you are top heavy on salaries and programmatically offer very little financial impact it may call into question the fidelity of the organization's mission. A budget for an organization is a plan and record of all the money that a company uses and earns. I say this explicitly so that as you continue to engage in this process that you always "make the numbers make sense".

The Master Budget

This budget accounts for every aspect of your organization. To build a master budget it is necessary to begin with the program budgets for each of the initiatives/programs/projects you have or will implement. You start at that level because it becomes an item(s) on the master budget.

The Program Budget

The program budget is a part of the master budget in a line item titled programming in most cases. This is a separate template used to delineate specific costs for each program. In these budgets you want to be as specific as possible. Oftentimes we are moving in hypotheticals for numbers that we can have actual concrete numbers for if we take the time to do the research. While prices can vary you can round up to ensure you have enough to cover potential fluctuations throughout the year. In this template I would also have a notes section where I enter the link and or how this line item is calculated especially when dealing with staffing. There are applications and software programs that can assist in documenting this information on a daily basis via manual input and automated transaction tracking. If you are just beginning a google sheet or excel can assist in getting this in a visual output necessary to begin bringing financial governance into full view. This is especially necessary when engaging your Board, staff and other members of your team in understanding their role in fundraising.

The Grant Budget

A grant budget is a financial plan that itemizes the costs of carrying out a specific program or project under a grant. It shows the funder the purpose and benefits of the grant, as well as the exact amount and time of the funding. A grant budget can be written using a template to make it clear and structured. While this sounds similar to the program budget it is not the same. This budget specifically speaks to the funding being requested in the grant proposal. This budget speaks to how the money will be spent in each category. For instance, if you have a grant where you are requesting $10,000 in the budget you can break down this request. Here is an example:

Summer Art Program - 20 Participants					
Item	Quantity	Cost	Grant Funds	Other Funds	Total
Personnel:					
Program Supervisor	1	$4000	$4000	0	$4000
Paid Intern	2	2000 x 2	$4000	0	$4000
Supplies:					
Bookbags	20	25x $20	$500	0	$500
Water Bottles	100 cases	20x $5	$500	0	$500
Art Kits	25	25 x 40	$1000	0	$1000
Total					$10,000

This table is just one of many examples of a grant budget. The other funds column is included as in many grants you will oftentimes have to identify if there is other funding available for the project. This can include other grants or in-kind donations that contribute to the project. In some cases there isn't any additional funding from other sources. Within a grant proposal this budget will drive your budget narrative. Everything you stipulate here will need an explanation. We will discuss this in more detail in the chapter to follow.

The Work

Nonprofit Leader

1. What are your nonprofit's current annual revenue and expenses?
2. Were any expenses in the previous year unnecessary?
3. How accurate were your revenue projections last year?
4. How much money do you have in reserve?
5. Is your donor base consistent or growing?
6. Does the organization have any liabilities or debt?
7. Create or Review and Update The Master Budget, The Program Budget(s). Use the following prompts to drive this process:

- **Review historical data:** Look at the previous year's budget and actual expenditures to understand patterns. Have you overspent consistently in certain categories?
- **Factor in inflation:** Be sure to account for the rate of inflation when calculating future expenses. This is especially relevant for costs like utilities, supplies, and rent.
- **Plan for the unexpected:** Make sure to leave some breathing room in your budget—and if you don't have operating reserves set aside for slow fundraising periods, consider adding a budget line to build your savings.
- **Collaborate with your team:** Gather feedback from staff members who are directly involved with the different programs or departments of your nonprofit. They'll be able to provide valuable input on potential expenses.

Grant Writer

1. Request the program budget from an organization you are writing for or create a program budget for a program you create from scratch. Review the program budget to see if there is anything missing. Ask yourself as you review the amount of money being requested in each line item enough to sustain the intended outcome of the program.
2. As you review the grant budget refer to the allowable costs section of the RFP and ensure that what is being requested is allowed.
3. Review the grant budget for timeline alignment and disbursement timelines. Identify when you will need the funds to be present.

Call To Action

Post a question on your social media asking the following question:

How much funding do you need to run a program for 50 participants for 3 hours a week?

This question will start a dialogue with your network that will provide you perspective on what you should be asking for programmatically. Feel free to adjust the question to fit your intended program. Once you receive the community perspective go back to your program budget and see how the funding amount compares.

CHAPTER TEN: The Budget Narrative

"A budget narrative is bringing the numbers to life

with words and more numbers"

-Jacqueleen Bido, EDD

The Story for Use

The budget narrative is where the numbers come to life in word form. This is where the funding grant reviewer will be able to align the intentions you described in your proposal, the funds you requested in your grant budget, and the reason you describe in the budget narrative. It is important that the requests outlined here are described in as much detail as possible yet concisely at the same time. This section will also be the time where you may go back to assess if this is enough for what you are saying you are going to do. This narrative has to make sense with the entire proposal.

There are varied presentations of budget narrative requirements. Some funders want brief descriptions while others may ask for purchasing quotes, shopping cart printouts, company project plans, job descriptions, etc. While these may not be as commonplace it is necessary to mention so that you are prepared. These documents can also assist in knowing what additional costs may be necessary for the grant to cover that often are overlooked like shipping costs, installation, and or upgrades and licenses for software upgrades.

The budget narrative should break down costs into words that explain how it will be implemented. Examples of this are as follows:

Art Kits: $1000.00

Each participant will be provided an art kit. The art kit will include canvas', crayons, markers, paint sets, art pencils, construction paper, book bag, water bottle, sketchbook, and paintbrushes. Each kit will cost $50 each. This kit will provide supplies enough for the 10-week summer eco-art program.

Paid Internship: 1000.00

There will be two paid internships with a stipend of 5000.00 dollars each. There will be a required 20 hours a week for 10 weeks to cover the needs of Farm-to Table Cooperative. These activities will include harvesting produce, packaging produce, disseminating to community members weekly, and data collection during produce pickups.

Refrigerated Van: $40,000

The purchase of the refrigerated van will support the proper safe transportation of produce from farm to packaging center. This van will increase the amount of produce that can be produced, harvested, and transported to local centers for fresh food access. This van will also serve as a method of expanding our reach throughout the City of Newark.

These are just some examples of narrative language as they all vary and should align to the program that you are requesting funding for. When the funding requests include construction there is a more delineated narrative that will include details that speak to the general contractor, architects, insurance, and other aspects of the project. This can be in conjunction with several projects within one proposal. The important part to remember is to not forget to include this in the narrative even if the construction budget is requested as a separate budget including the grant budget. As stated in other chapters while this is the recommendation, always follow what is requested in the RFP, NOFO, Grant Guidelines to ensure you are submitting a complete proposal.

The Work

Nonprofit Leader

Take your program budget and for each item and write the rationale behind the requested item in alignment with the program.

If you have a team meaning more than you show them your narrative and have a discussion about what has been written. This allows for your team to also understand how the program budget and the items listed drive the outcome.

Grant Writer

Request the program budget from the organization you write for and for each item write the rationale behind the requested item in alignment with the program. The ability to explain the financial request is an integral practice. This information can come from your point of contact at the organization or information you already know because you assisted or developed the program yourself.

Once you have completed this process, review the narrative for alignment to the proposal. Ask yourself, do the requested items drive the outcome of the program, the funder's expected outcomes, and the fiscal need to be successful? Review this with your organization's point of contact as needed.

Call to Action

Read the budget narrative. Post on your social media the reason you feel it is important to give back to the community through the program you wrote the narrative for. Tag me and 3 people in your post.

CHAPTER ELEVEN: The Funders

"You cannot receive what you don't give.
Outflow determines inflow."
-Eckhart Tolle

When it comes to grants, The Funders are an integral part of grants and the nonprofit sector. Many funders have been the financial lifeline for impact locally, nationally, and globally. It is important to know:

- Who they are?
- What they value?
- What about what you value in the programming and projects you bring forth align with their values?
- What do you know about them, their staff, their impact?

Understanding this and all you can about the funder will help you understand what kind of programming or initiatives they will be interested in funding. It is also important as you engage in this chapter to understand in what ways this money is navigated to and throughout the communities they impact on every level.

Grant Funders

1. Foundation Grants

    - Private and public foundations and charities create these grant opportunities.
    - There are thousands of foundation grants available. However, most aren't publicly available.
    - Each grant will have various requirements and are available to nonprofits, businesses and individuals.

2. Corporate Grants

    - Many corporations make grant funds available to meet a wide range of needs.
    - These can be available to nonprofits, businesses and individuals.
    - In most cases, corporations also tend to set aside money at the beginning of the fiscal year and host competitions to distribute funds.

3. Federal Government Grants

    - Federal grants draw from U.S. federal tax revenue and budget allocations.
    - They do not offer "free money" to individuals or businesses, only loans and social welfare benefits.
    - In addition, the federal government only gives grants to states and organizations to stimulate the national economy.

4. State Government Grants
    - In fact, these recipients generally include nonprofit organizations, schools, municipalities and research labs.
    - Usually, these grants are only for organizations working with government-funded programs and projects.
    - Also, by the nature of their smaller scope, state government grants are smaller than federal grants.

5. Local City Government Grants
    - City governments and municipalities create these grants.
    - The grants are intended to directly stimulate the community around them.
    - Typically, these grants are also available to nonprofits, businesses and individuals..

Have you heard of Donor-Advised Funds (DAF)?

Donor- Advised Funds (DAF)

A donor-advised fund, or DAF, is an account where you can deposit assets for donation to charity over time.

The donor gets a tax deduction for making contributions to the donor-advised fund.

A sponsoring organization manages the account; the donor recommends how to invest the assets and where to donate them. Technically, once assets are deposited into a donor-advised fund, the sponsoring organization has legal control over them. But as long as you choose a charity that's recognized by the IRS as a U.S. charitable organization, the sponsoring organization will usually use your charities of choice.

How Well Do You Know Them?

Quite often when it comes to the funders that exist in our local, national, and global community many of us do not know who they are. In some cases the only time we do find out anything about them is when funding in alignment with our cause or causes is released. This is one of the habits I hope to eradicate as I continue this journey in grant writing. I hope you do the same as well because knowing our potential funders is so very important. Many of the funders are seeking to understand the needs of a given community. They want to direct their funds to areas that increase the impact and or address the root causes of the problem. When we don't seek to understand who they are we miss out on the opportunity to highlight for them the issues that may go unnoticed locally, nationally, and globally.

This is done a couple of ways but lets begin with utilizing the internet. I run searches on local foundations, funders, and corporate entities both government and private institutions. When I populate the list I want to get to know I look at their website, I look to see if they have ever funded anyone in the area of my cause, I make sure to subscribe to them.

On a government level you must get to know your political constituency and in my opinion those who are in the planning department. I say this because any federal funding forthcoming or currently available is not unknown to these stakeholders. It is how the local government funds various programs throughout the city, county or state. The planning department is important as well because it highlights forthcoming projects and infrastructure of the community. Your organization may be able to fulfill a need within those plans. Often there are block grants that offer nonprofits the funding to support the attainment of building, land, etc. Usually, funding like this is aligned to a federal funding act where the state or city is a passthrough for funding. You can subscribe to city, county, and state websites as well.

We should not forget about institutions of learning and healthcare systems that also serve as pass through institutions for funding opportunities. These institutions have their own strategic goals as well as research collaboration opportunities. There are a host of departments that will align with your organizational goals and or offer opportunities to bring your organizational service and expertise to their staff. Examples of this look like nutrition classes, community beautification through volunteerism, and subject matter expertise from local stakeholders. In addition, the opportunity to collaborate on the development of programmatic offerings as majors and or certificate programs in universities. You can subscribe to these entities as well.

In all cases the aforementioned is only as successful as your implementation and consistency.

The Work
Nonprofit Leader
Block off two hours of your day in any increment of time. For one week research your local funders. Create a list of the funders whose funding goals are similar to that of your organization or program. Subscribe to each of them. In some cases you may want to schedule a meet and greet virtually or in person to introduce yourself and your organization.

Grant Writer

Block off two hours of your day in any increment of time. For one week research your local funders. Create a list of the funders whose funding goals are similar to that of the organization you write for. Subscribe to each of them. In some cases you may want to schedule a meet and greet virtually or in person to introduce yourself and understand their funding focus and opportunities for collaboration.

Call To Action

Select a local funder to highlight on your social media. Tag 1 or more organizations or stakeholders who can benefit from the funders opportunity.

CHAPTER TWELVE: The Funding

"If you think having uncomfortable conversations with donors is hard,
just wait until you see what happens when you don't."
- Mallory Erickson

There are several types of funding that exist on a local, state, national, and at times global level. These types of funding come with various different requirements for eligibility which will be important for you to always understand for any grant opportunity. Funding comes in large amounts and in small amounts. One of the things that has always sustained me through my grant writing journey is that any amount of money for the good of the people can make a difference when implemented with the people in mind. I remember the first grant benign for $2000 dollars. It was like we had hit the lottery. The next was for $10,000 dollars and so forth the amounts grew. We knew how to implement the funding and our ability to collaborate to make an impact. Don't look down on small amounts of money. What you must do is look at the bandwidth needed to bring forth programming with fidelity. All money isn't good money and that is ever present when applying for certain kinds of grants. Some funding comes with little reporting while others have so many reporting requirements that it entails the dedication of a full-time staff member. Keep all these things in mind as you seek funding.

15 Different Types of Funding

Government Grants

A government grant is a financial award given by a federal, state, or local government authority for a beneficial project. Government grants help fund ideas and projects providing public services and stimulating the economy. These grants can be researched and traditionally applied on grants.gov or the state or local government are the passthrough entities where you will submit your application to them directly. If you are submitting to the State or Local entity there will usually be a separate RFP released to direct your steps. In all cases start with grant.gov for government grant opportunities and required funding documents.

Foundation Grants

Foundation grants come from philanthropic organizations (like families, private groups, public groups, faith-based organizations, or community funds) to help advance causes or nonprofits in a specific locale. There are foundations that serve local initiatives and other national initiatives. In some cases Foundation Grants require a Letter of Intent (LOI) which gives the funder the number of potential applicants, funding amount being requested, and a brief summary of the program. In addition, some Foundation Grants are by invitation only which affirms previous recommendations about getting to know the foundations in your area.

Corporate Grants

A corporate grant is a financial award given by a company or organization to an individual, group, or organization for a specific purpose, such as research or charitable purposes. Corporate grants can vary in size, scope, and purpose, and may be given in the form of cash, in-kind services, or other resources.

Non-Profit Pass-Through Grants

Pass-through grants are a type of federal funding that is awarded to one organization, which then distributes the funds--or passes them through--to another organization or individual for the purpose of carrying out a specific project or program. These types of grants are commonly used in situations where the grant-making agency wants to provide funding to organizations that are not eligible to receive grants directly, or where the agency wants to support a specific project or program but does not have the staff or expertise to manage it directly.

Research Grants

Research grants are financial awards provided by various funding sources, such as government agencies, non-profit organizations, corporations, and foundations, to support research projects conducted by individual researchers, research teams, or institutions. Research grants offer you an opportunity to evaluate your own program in collaboration with independent researchers and or institutions of learning.

Educational Grants

The Department of Education has funds available to help state education agencies (SEAs), local education agencies (LEAs), and other education stakeholders to support state and local efforts to improve student achievement, educational equity, and access to educational opportunities for all students.

Arts and Culture Grants

Arts and culture grants refer to grant opportunities designed to fund organizations and programs working to support the proliferation of artistic expression and creativity within a community and/or to preserve and celebrate a community's culture, including its heritage, customs, and art.

Small Business Grants

Small business grants are sums of money given for a particular purpose by government or nonprofit organizations for economic and business development. Unlike small-business loans, grants offer access to capital that doesn't need to be repaid. Small business grants are available from several entities, including the federal government, state and local governments, and private corporations. There are four types of grants available to business owners: federal grants, state grants, local grants, and corporate grants.

Environmental Grants

are designed to empower nonprofits, charities, and community organizations to implement projects that address environmental issues. These grants support projects related to conservation, sustainable agriculture, renewable energy, and environmental education.

Humanitarian and Social Services Grants

Humanitarian and Social Services Grants12345 support programs and nonprofits addressing social issues like poverty, healthcare access, disaster relief, food security, and equal rights14. These grants are usually funded by corporations and health foundations14. Government grants are also a primary source of funding for humanitarian relief projects3.

Community Development Grants

Grants for community development are funds that support projects and initiatives that improve the social, economic, and environmental conditions of communities.Some sources of grants for community development are Local governments, such as councils, that provide funding for local projects and programs Community foundations, that offer place-based funding and networking opportunities International organizations and foundations, that offer grants for specific regions, themes, or sectors, such as security, human rights, or education. Some examples are the Sub-Saharan Africa Security Sector Consortium, the Ireland Fellows Programme, and the Gupta Family Foundation.

Technology and Innovation Grants

Technology and innovation grants include programs like SBIR and STTR, which fund startups and small businesses in technology areas to stimulate innovation and meet federal research and development needs. Additionally, grants are available for various entities, including states, Indian Tribes, cities, and economic development organizations, with a focus on improving science, technology, innovation, or entrepreneurship.

Matching Grants

Matching grants are grants provided by corporations, foundations, or individuals to nonprofit organizations wherein the corporation agrees to match a certain amount of money that the nonprofit raises. Matching grants require your nonprofit to contribute to your fund like the grantor does. When applying for a matching grant, you'll agree to contribute a specific amount to your own campaign.

Capacity Building Grants

Capacity-Building grant is a sum of money that a foundation offers to a nonprofit to work on new strategies, develop competencies and improve processes and systems around efficiency. With this type of support, nonprofits can move into a position where they have a greater capacity to serve others. Capacity-building can help nonprofits to:

Strengthen competencies

Enhance internal processes

Improve leadership

Provide staff training

Procure technology

Seed Grants

Seed grants are small amounts of money invested in research projects and teams at the earliest stages of development. These funds allow researchers to advance their teaming efforts and/or to obtain preliminary data demonstrating the potential viability of the work. Often, seed projects lead to extramural research opportunities and funding.

Nonprofit Revenue Streams

Throughout the lifetime of a nonprofit there are several revenue streams that sustain the nonprofit financially. Establishing multiple revenue streams is imperative for those who seek to be around for the long term.

Fees for Services and Sales of Products

According to the National Center for Charitable Statistics, such sources of revenue provided almost half (47.5 percent) of the total revenue for public charities (501c3) in 2013. Another quarter of revenues came from government contracts for services.

Charitable Contributions

Although the total income for nonprofits comes from an assortment of sources, of which contributions are a part, individuals are the largest source of charitable donations for nonprofit charitable organizations.

According to Giving USA, total charitable giving in the U.S. reached more than $427.71 billion in 2018. Of that amount, 68 percent came from individuals. The rest of the philanthropic pie consisted of government and foundation grants, bequests, and corporate philanthropy. Charitable nonprofits (also called public charities or 501c3) especially depend on donations from a lot of individuals. That is partly because public charities are required to receive a large part of their support from the public. That public support helps qualify them fortax-exemption by the IRS.

Corporate Philanthropy

Corporate philanthropy has come to be an integral part of the identity of most large corporations and many smaller businesses as well. Corporate social responsibility (CSR) has become more important as consumers have become more likely to buy from socially responsible companies. Corporate funding can be a long-term commitment to specific causes and the charities connected to them, or it can be more episodic and market-driven, revolving around particular campaigns, events, and projects. Funding from corporations can be a good source of support for new initiatives, special programs, and special events. Nonprofits increasingly look for opportunities to form corporate partnerships for sponsorships and cause-related marketing. Companies also often help their employees give to charities and even match those contributions. Employee volunteer programs are popular, and some grants are tied to employee volunteer hours.

Federal, State, and Local Governments

Many nonprofits benefit from all levels of government. Prominent examples are public education, higher education, and public media. Federal, state, and local government grants fund many programs provided by nonprofits, especially for human service and healthcare. Grants.gov provides up-to-date information and a directory of federal grants.

Federated Funds

Community-based efforts such as United Way, United Arts, and community funds can be reliable sources of relatively large amounts of money. Federated funds have traditionally thrived because they supported employee giving at companies. Today, they have become less popular as new ways of employee giving have been established and as younger donors, such as millennials, seek to be more involved with the charities to which they give.

Grant-Making Public Charities

Public charities are a cross between a private foundation and a charity. They typically receive funding from the general public, government, and private foundations. They may perform public service, but primarily raise funds and provide grants to other nonprofits that provide direct service. You can find many such grant-making public charities in your local area. Some are linked to a national organization; the Junior League is one such example. Grant-making public charities file IRS Form 990, so information about them can be found in many databases, such as at the Foundation Center and GuideStar.

Foundations

Foundations come in various sizes and types, but their grants can be substantial and significant. Corporate foundations are private foundations, but their boards are often made up of corporate officers. Their endowment funds exist separately from the corporation, and they have their own professional staff. Family foundations receive endowments from individuals or families. Many large family foundations have been around a long time and become household names. Think of the Gates Foundation, the Rockefeller Foundation, and the Ford Foundation. Numerous family foundations have endowments in the billions, but most family foundations are much smaller, tend to fund locally, and often have little to no professional staff. These types of foundations usually give money to their hometown charities. Community foundations are public foundations that pool the assets of many donors. They work to improve their local communities through grantmaking, awarding scholarships, and providing services to donors. Community foundations have become very active in providing donor-advised funds for donors who want to become more purposeful in their giving but don't want to set up their own private foundations. Community foundations today often organize giving days
to help local nonprofits raise funds.

Recurring vs. Episodic Funding

Besides seeking support from a variety of sources, your fundraising
program should find both ongoing financial support and episodic
support. Recurring funds can be counted on year to year, while episodic
funding occurs at irregular times.

Recurring support usually comes through programs and activities such
as the Annual Fund. An annual fund means just that—annual (or more
frequent) appeals to a core group of constituents. Such funds are usually

unrestricted—available for any use—and may represent a significant percentage of a nonprofit's annual income.

Monthly giving programs also have proven their worth for charities. These are sometimes called sustainer programs to which donors pledge contributions on a regular schedule.

Sales of Products and Services. Some nonprofits own stores or provide services that can represent a substantial income stream. The Girl Scouts is one obvious example with its annual sale of cookies, and Goodwill Industries is probably the largest nonprofit retailer. A symphony or the theater earns income through the sale of tickets. However, earned income must be related to the mission of the organization, or it can be taxed as unrelated business income.

Multi Year Grants. A grant-giving organization such as a foundation may provide restricted funding for a particular program or, more rarely, unrestricted funding to help cover the overhead costs of running the organization.

Endowment Income. Many large nonprofits, notably higher education institutions, and healthcare organizations build up significant endowment funds that produce interest that supports their programs. Endowments are restricted with only the investment interest allowed to be spent from year to year.

Episodic funding may come from a foundation or corporate grants, special events, or a bequest. These funds may be restricted or unrestricted.

Two Special Types of Fundraising

A capital campaign is a time-limited effort by a nonprofit organization to raise significant dollars for a particular project, such as:

Funding a new building

Raising funds for a specific project, such as cancer research Increasing one specific asset such as an endowment

Capital campaigns have a beginning and an end but often span several years. A capital campaign employs all the usual means of raising funds such as direct mail and direct solicitation. Capital campaigns require extensive preparation and skillful execution.

Most nonprofits now have planned giving programs that help donors include their favorite causes in their wills or estate planning. The charitable gift annuity has become quite popular among many donors as it allows tax advantages while providing income during the donor's lifetime.

An effective fundraising plan includes a balance of these techniques and sources. Establishing unrestricted, ongoing funding is the most critical task, followed by other funding that will grow the organization and ensure its future.

The Work

Nonprofit Leader

For each of the following types of funding search for an available grant. Once you have identified the available grant, save the link or write down the website you found it on. Once you have compiled a list of grants take time to see which ones align to your organization or programmatic offering. This will help you see opportunities in various funding types.

Government Grants

Foundation Grants

Corporate Grants

Non-Profit Pass-Through Grants

Research Grants

Educational Grants

Arts and Culture Grants

Small Business Grants

Environmental Grants

Humanitarian and Social Services Grants

Community Development Grants

Technology and Innovation Grants

Matching Grants

Capacity Building Grants

Seed Grants

Grant Writer

For each of the following types of funding search for an available grant. Once you have identified the available grant, save the link or write down the website you found it on. Once you have compiled a list of grants take time to see which ones align organization or programmatic offering for the organization you write for. This can be more than one organization. This will help you see opportunities in various funding types.

Government Grants

Foundation Grants

Corporate Grants

Non-Profit Pass-Through Grants

Research Grants

Educational Grants

Arts and Culture Grants

Small Business Grants

Environmental Grants

Humanitarian and Social Services Grants

Community Development Grants

Technology and Innovation Grants

Matching Grants

Capacity Building Grants

Seed Grants

Call To Action

For the grants you have identified, take a couple of them and post them on your social media and tag an organization of your choosing. This habit of sharing resources is integral in grassroots environments. This also increases the possibility for other entities to tag you when there are grants or other resources available. In the end I believe in the power of reciprocation.

CHAPTER THIRTEEN: The Accounting

Accounting is the language of business."
- Warren Buffett

What is Financial Accountability?

This speaks directly to how the organization accounts for money. Specifically, how:

it comes into the organization. accounted for via ledger or accounting application

it is kept and accessed Most important…. HOW IS IT SPENT!

4 Financial Statements Nonprofits Must Keep

Statement of Financial Position - This document is also known as a balance sheet.Nonprofit balance sheets list your organization's assets, liabilities, and net assets.

Statement of Financial Position
As at 30 June 2021

	Note	Actual 2021 $000	Budget 2021 $000	Actual 2020 $000
ASSETS				
Current Assets				
Cash and cash equivalents	4	3,659	43	2,912
Trade and other receivables	5	175	150	300
Inventories		92	100	87
		3,926	293	3,299
Non-Current Assets				
Property, Plant and Equipment	6	-	-	-
		-	-	-
TOTAL ASSETS		3,926	293	3,299
LIABILITIES				
Current Liabilities				
Trade,other payables and accruals	7	1,016	628	545
Monies held in trust	7	9	-	9
Revenue in Advance	8	468	-	661
Employee Benefits	9	401	380	562
		1,894	1,008	1,777
TOTAL LIABILITIES		1,894	1,008	1,777
NET ASSETS		2,032	(715)	1,522
EQUITY				
Accumulated Comprehensive revenue and expense	10	224	(2,037)	242
Restricted Funds	11	1,808	1,322	1,280
TOTAL EQUITY		2,032	(715)	1,522

The accompanying notes form part of these financial statements

The budget figures are derived from the Statement of Intent as approved by the Board at the beginning of the financial year. Where required these figures have been broken down further for comparative purposes. Refer to Note 16 and Note 19 for explanations of major variances.

2. Statement of Activities - Nonprofits use the statement of activities to review changes to their net assets and show revenue and expenses over the accounting year.

CODE FOR SCIENCE AND SOCIETY, INC.

STATEMENTS OF ACTIVITIES

For the years ended June 30, 2021 and 2020

	June 30, 2021			June 30, 2020		
	Without Donor Restrictions	With Donor Restrictions	Total	Without Donor Restrictions	With Donor Restrictions	Total
REVENUES AND SUPPORT						
Grants and contributions revenue	$ 2,675	$ 5,501,175	$ 5,503,850	$ 1,035	$ 2,909,984	$ 2,911,019
Contract revenue	-	145,648	145,648	-	186,493	186,493
Other revenue	-	3,529	3,529	-	2,380	2,380
Net assets released from restrictions	3,607,571	(3,607,571)	-	1,767,118	(1,767,118)	-
TOTAL REVENUES AND SUPPORT	3,610,246	2,042,781	5,653,027	1,758,153	1,331,739	3,099,892
EXPENSES						
Program services	2,992,452	-	2,992,452	1,474,890	-	1,474,890
Fundraising	215,756	-	215,756	126,881	-	126,881
Management and general	215,350	-	215,350	79,488	-	79,488
TOTAL EXPENSES	3,423,558	-	3,423,558	1,681,259	-	1,681,259
CHANGE IN NET ASSETS BEFORE FORGIVENESS OF LOAN	186,688	2,042,781	2,229,469	86,894	1,331,739	1,418,633
FORGIVENESS OF LOAN	63,475	98,647	162,122	-	-	-
CHANGE IN NET ASSETS	250,163	2,141,428	2,391,591	86,894	1,331,739	1,418,633
NET ASSETS, BEGINNING OF YEAR	195,233	1,911,108	2,106,341	108,339	579,369	687,708
NET ASSETS, END OF YEAR	$ 445,396	$ 4,052,536	$ 4,497,932	$ 195,233	$ 1,911,108	$ 2,106,341

The accompanying notes are an integral part of these financial statements.

5

3. Statement of Cash Flow - The statement of cash flow shows how cash moves in and out of a nonprofit. Board members and other leaders can use this statement for better insight into how much is available to pay expenses.

CODE FOR SCIENCE AND SOCIETY, INC.

STATEMENTS OF CASH FLOWS

For the years ended June 30, 2021 and 2020

	2021	2020
CASH FLOWS FROM OPERATING ACTIVITIES:		
Change in net assets	$ 2,391,591	$ 1,418,633
Adjustment to reconcile change in net assets to net cash provided by operating activities:		
Forgiveness of loan payable	(160,800)	-
Change in operating assets and liabilities:		
Grants and accounts receivable	(385,798)	(92,671)
Accounts payable	109,747	16,638
Accrued liabilities	(3,986)	3,986
Grants payable	91,000	(80,000)
NET CASH PROVIDED BY OPERATING ACTIVITIES	2,041,754	1,266,586
CASH FLOWS FROM FINANCING ACTIVITIES:		
Proceeds from loan payable	-	160,800
NET CASH PROVIDED BY FINANCING ACTIVITIES	-	160,800
NET INCREASE IN CASH AND CASH EQUIVALENTS	2,041,754	1,427,386
CASH AND CASH EQUIVALENTS, BEGINNING OF YEAR	2,162,575	735,189
CASH AND CASH EQUIVALENTS, END OF YEAR	$ 4,204,329	$ 2,162,575

SUPPLEMENTAL CASH FLOW:

Noncash financing activities include forgiveness of Paycheck Protection Program loan of $160,800 and related interest of $1,322 included in income during the year ending June 30, 2021.

4. Statement of Functional Expenses -

The statement of functional expenses gives donors more details on how the organization spends funds. The IRS requires nonprofits to include this statement when filing Form 990.

CODE FOR SCIENCE AND SOCIETY, INC.

STATEMENTS OF FUNCTIONAL EXPENSES

For the years ended June 30, 2021 and 2020

	June 30, 2021				June 30, 2020			
	Program Services	Fundraising	Management and General	Total Expenses	Program Services	Fundraising	Management and General	Total Expenses
Salaries and related benefits	$ 1,335,964	$ 146,447	$ 49,446	$ 1,531,857	$ 1,003,967	$ 106,618	$ 29,238	$ 1,139,823
Professional services	823,305	67,416	151,864	1,042,585	367,612	16,168	37,668	421,448
Web services	57,237	636	6,230	64,103	43,073	506	4,713	48,292
Office expenses	10,259	666	1,076	12,001	13,832	1,363	2,551	17,746
Travel	-	-	1,984	1,984	16,783	1,573	2,518	20,874
Program events and marketing	7,127	-	-	7,127	15,537	-	280	15,817
Grants	759,585	-	-	759,585	8,000	-	-	8,000
Insurance	3,538	588	2,262	6,388	4,345	653	1,118	6,116
Other expenses (income), net	(4,563)	3	2,488	(2,072)	1,741	-	1,402	3,143
TOTAL FUNCTIONAL EXPENSES	$ 2,992,452	$ 215,756	$ 215,350	$ 3,423,558	$ 1,474,890	$ 126,881	$ 79,488	$ 1,681,259

NONPROFIT AUDIT

A nonprofit audit examines financial records, bank accounts, business transactions, accounting principles, and internal controls within a nonprofit organization. A nonprofit audit can be required from some funders. While the word "Audit" is intimidating there is nothing to worry about when you have proper compliance in place for how money is managed within your organization. For grant writers this is not technically under your control but can be a discussion or a resource you provide to the organization you write for.

The Work
Nonprofit Leader

Develop or request from the person responsible for the organization's finances he requested documentation. If you do not have a financial compliance plan in place, develop one with your team. The processes created in your plan should be implemented real-time.

Grant Writer

Research a nonprofit audit process. Look for a nonprofit financial compliance resource. This will make you well versed in the product.

Call To Action

Create a post on your social media that highlights the 4 required financial documents nonprofit should have. This will assist other organizations as they grow and engage in their nonprofit journey.

CHAPTER FOURTEEN: Summary

Nonprofit Leader

Dear Nonprofit Leader,

At this point in the book you are realizing everything you are bringing to fruition and or understanding the preparation necessary to do so. You are realizing the importance of your programming and the \ost of impact. If you are in the space where your programming is established you are asking yourself important questions like where do we go from here? Or How else can this program bring about increased collaboration and or resources? You may be feeling the pressures of financial sustainability but to this I tell you to identify and develop all of your revenue streams and work on becoming a subject matter expert on the need you seek to impact. The money will go when the programming is sound and don't ever forget to shout it from the hilltop when you are making a difference in your community and the people you serve.

Grant Writer

Dear Grant Writer,

At this point you are realizing the many areas that go into writing a proposal for an organization. There is a consistency on your part to continuously build your knowledge around nonprofit governance because it helps support your understanding of how the organization functions or should function. There will be times where you will develop programming in alignment with the organization's mission and capabilities in order to submit a successful grant. It is necessary for you to build your own capacity via this book and other resources that exist. You are not simply a grant writer but you are the bridge between the organization and the founder to build these connections for overall community impact. I chose grant writing because it is how I give back to the community. When you get to know the founders and the funding streams it assists you in understanding how to write for a specific grant. Now is the time to network both on social media and in your local community or state. I you don't know accounting or

The budget makes you nervous to seek a mentor. I know for the areas I didn't understand fully I sought out the subject matter experts in that area. Now is the time to believe in yourself and your abilities.

PART THREE: The Grant Proposal

"The first draft is just you telling yourself the story."
— Terry Pratchett

CHAPTER FIFTEEN: From LOI to RFP to the Proposal

"If you don't have time to read, you don't have the
time (or the tools) to write. Simple as that."
-Stephen King

What is an LOI?

An LOI is commonly known as a Letter of Intent, Interest, or Inquiry. is a formal request of a nonprofit organization that seeks financing for its charitable purposes.

This document is requested by the funder before you are able to submit the full proposal to:

To anticipate the number of grant proposals that will be submitted to manage the review team..

To weed through the organizations and initiatives may not be a fit for a full proposal submission.

Some funders make LOI's a mandatory submission dictated by an LOI deadline separate from the grant proposal deadline. If you miss the LOI deadline in some cases you will not be allowed to apply for the grant at all.

What is included in an LOI?

- an introduction to your project,
- contact information at your agency,
- a description of your organization,
- a statement of need,
- your methodology and/or an achievable solution to the need,
- a brief discussion of other funding sources,
- as well as a final summary.

LOI Best Practices

1. Keep it short - The LOI should be brief, one-page or the allotted amount by the funder. It is considered an informative letter that summarizes your ultimate proposal.

2. The structure of the LOI is a business letter - it should be directed to the specific name of the recipient on your organization's letterhead.

3. Be seccint without missing the point - the information you provide should be enticing information that inspires the reader to continue reading.

Most importantly, be meticulous in following the directions provided by the funding source.

Think of an LOI as a "pre-proposal." If the funding source likes what they read, it will help your organization to get noticed.

What is a Request for Proposal (RFP)?

Grantmakers, whether a foundation, government or the funding entity, customarily release a Request for Proposal (RFP) ahead of a grant the grant submission deadline. There are occasions where there is no RFP release but guidelines for the grant can be found online the grantmakers website. This is the most important document to have and read as it governs every step of the submission process. This document will provide vital information to include grant submission technical support when available other resources to support your understanding of the funder as well as expectations and timelines for submission and award announcements. Whenever you are WRITING MAKE SURE TO DOWNLOAD AND REFERENCE THIS DOCUMENT FREQUENTLY.

RFP Best Practices

1. READ THE RFP - Do not begin writing without reading the RFP.
2. Know your deadline - RFP's have deadlines that close at 11:59pm on a given date and others are at 5:00pm.
3. Know your Eligibility Requirements - Each grant has a different requirement to apply that will either include or exclude your organization.
4. Know the Funding timeline- Grant funding periods can vary from 6 months to 3 years and are governed by the individual funder.
5. Follow the format requested - This is not the time to be creative, if say the specific font, font size and page number, follow it. There are grant review boards that will not give you the benefit of the doubt and disqualify your submission for not following the requested format.

Finding Grant Opportunities

Grant opportunities can be found in a number of places. My method is by understanding the funders in my location and subscribing to their information. There are platforms that for free or a fee track a host of grant opportunities. These platforms can be subscribed to as well. One of my favorites is Philanthropy News Digest www.philanthropynewsdigest.org . The way the information is presented is very user friendly and on their site you can look at specific grant categories and states. There are other paid platforms that offer an array of opportunities as well like Grant Watch https://www.grantwatch.com/grantnews/grants/. I still subscribe to these for the information they share. For those of you who may not have the finances to pay for a subscription to a specific platform you can ultimately use the information presented in email news announcements and run an internet search for that specific grant or funder. Nothing can stop you from obtaining the information you need when you take the time to find it.

There are certain registrations you will need in order to complete the required SAM.gov UEI registration in order to apply for government grants. The following registrations are in best practice to have:

Dun & Bradstreet Number

Obtaining a Dun & Bradstreet D-U-N-S Number is simple and free. Short for Data Universal Numbering System, a D-U-N-S Number is a unique nine-digit identifier for businesses. It can open many doors for your company, giving you the opportunity to partner with other businesses, receive to submit contract bids, and more.

https://www.dnb.com/en-us/smb/duns/get-a-duns.html

Systems of Awards Management (SAM) Unique Entity Identifier UEI

The SAM Unique Entity ID is a 12-character alphanumeric ID assigned to an entity by SAM.gov. New entities can get their Unique Entity ID at SAM.gov and complete an entity registration. You do not have to pay for this registration as on SAM.gov it is free. There are several resources to guide you through the process and customer service that can assist you as well. Be mindful as there are companies that will charge you to complete this registration. Again you do not have to use a third party for this process. This registration is necessary as **YOU CANNOT APPLY FOR A GRANT ON GRANTS.GOV WITHOUT AN ACTIVE UEI.** You will also have to complete a SAM UEI Renewal every year. It is important to keep this in mind as you seek to apply for government funding. Renewals can be quick or take an extended amount of time at different times throughout the year.

Grants.gov

This Is the home of government funding. Before you continue reading go to www.grants.gov and create a profile. Grants.gov is a free online source for finding and applying for federal grants. It provides access to more than 1,000 federal grant programs with approximately $500 billion in awards annually. This site is updated often and as stated before is one of the sites you should search frequently as part of your routine. There are a host of topics and funding areas that may interest you or drive your future collaboration with local and statewide stakeholders.

The Grant Proposal

The grant proposal as mentioned prior is guided by the request for proposal, notice of funding, or proposal guidelines. Every aspect of what is requested will become your proposal. Keep in mind that depending on the submission platform used by the funder the proposal may be submitted in sections, via separate questions in the submission portal, or via document upload. Be mindful that you don't forget to submit a requested document as it can look differently from written form to actual online submission. The grant proposal when answered in separate questions online may have character or work limitations. This is important to note as it can drastically change your answers. As a habit, always log onto to see the layout of the submission questions and character or word limitations. Please note the difference between character and word limits:

Character Limitations: Every letter, number, grammatical symbols, and special symbols count.

Example: The world is a great place. = 27 characters

Word Limitations: Every word counts and the count is triggered by each space.

Example: The world is a great place. = 6 words

The first time I learned this lesson was for one grant I had to adjust the organizational history from 250 words to 300 characters. This was a test of cutting out every word that I thought was necessary and overall concept and extrapolating the most poignant parts of the organization's history. This is where your ability to get straight to the point will help you make these adjustments. It is also necessary to be able to relinquish the statement, phrases, or words you have fallen in love with. The more you write grants there are statements you can essentially use as template language. While templated language you use consistently is in best practice don't lose sight of the main points you must get across in your overall proposal as they will vary from grant to grant. The following chapters will provide you with an overall understanding of the various parts of a proposal. While all parts may not be included or requested in every proposal it is important for you to have a working understanding of them.

For every chapter to follow you will want to create a version of the section writing topic for your own organization and as a grant writer for the organization you write for.

CHAPTER SIXTEEN: Abstract and Statement of Need

"Find a need and fill it."
- Ruth Stafford Peale

How to Write an Abstract Proposal

An Abstract can be considered the snapshot for what you are presenting in your grant proposal. The following list are things to include:

- Project background
- Specific aims, objectives, or hypotheses
- Significance of the proposed research or project
- Relevance to the mission of the funding agency
- Unique features
- Methodology (action steps) to be used
- Expected results
- Evaluation methods or how will success be determined
- How your results will affect other research areas or community needs
- The abstract should be concise and no longer than a page

Technical vs Non-Technical

When writing an Abstract and proposal it is imperative that you keep your audience in mind. There are ways to write Technical Abstracts and Non-Technical Abstracts.

In Technical Abstracts the:

- writing assumes background knowledge
- Few justifications
- Extensive use of terminology
- Few definitions and examples

Non-Technical Abstracts

- Require background
- Frequent initial purpose clauses
- Terminology is used with caution
- More definitions and examples

Things to Avoid in Your Abstract

When writing your abstract there are things to avoid. First your descriptions of past accomplishments should not be referenced at this time. It should not be written in first person. Do not present any information that is not covered in your proposal. This abstract is providing a snapshot of what you are writing about in your proposal. Never include confidential information, graphs, images, or citations. This is a very high-level depiction of what you will provide detail for in the actual proposal.

Abstract Structure Writing Prompts

When you think about the Problem:

- It has not been determined if/that (Enter Problem)
- is unclear that the (Enter Problem) is limited by
- The question remains if (Enter Problem)

When you think about the Objectives:

- Our objective is to (Enter Objective)
- We propose to (Enter Objective)
- We will examine the hypothesis that (Enter Objective)

When you think about the Strategy:

- We will achieve this goal by (Enter Strategy)
- Specifically, we will (Enter Strategy)
- by (Enter Strategy)
- Our general strategy is to (Enter Strategy)

When you think about the Significance:

- is important for (Enter Significance)
- These results may play a role in (Enter Significance)
- will provide insights into (Enter Significance)

Implementation Activity

Now complete the following prompts about a program you intend to implement:

- It has not been determined if/that (Enter Problem)
- Our objective is to (Enter Objective)
- Specifically, we will (Enter Strategy)
- will provide insights into (Enter Significance)

Once you have entered the information in the aforementioned writing prompts fill in additional sentences to evolve the Problem, Objectives, Strategy, and Significance as outlined at the beginning of this chapter.

How to Write a Strong Needs Statement

To begin we must understand that an Abstract and a Statement of Need are two different things. While they have similar elements an Abstract in most cases will never be more than one page. A statement of need often ranges from one page to 3 pages but as stated many times in this book, align your writing and number of pages to the RFP/NOFO. At its foundation a needs statement has to be written from a place that paints a vivid concise picture of the problem. This is where all of the topics we discussed earlier in the chapter support the writing of a solid needs statement. This statement of need begins to drive the narrative to the problems and proposed solutions you are highlighting that will begin directing how you write the remainder of the proposal.

Statement of Need

To write a successful needs statement begins by describing the main issue. The main issue should be focused on a single overarching problem in the community. While there are many problems in the community, be mindful that you focus on one core concern and any other issues tied to the core concern can be discussed briefly if necessary. Ensure the statement focuses on the community you serve as an organization while presenting the challenge at hand and make it real to the donor. If the RFP allows for the targeting of multiple concerns, write in alignment to the RFP. For example, when applying for a medical research grant, write a statement that focuses on a niche in medical research that needs to be filled. The core concern should be a gap in medical research in a given field and other issues should be discussed briefly. Whether a medical research need or a food security concern the same strategy applies.

Provide statistics and data

Remember earlier we spoke about research and data. Reference those chapters as you continue to write your proposal. Quantitative data includes numbers and facts, while qualitative data includes interviews, stories, and public opinions. Statistics and data help in providing concrete evidence to support the statement. In addition, statistics help in comparing the current status with the desired status. Recent data and reliable sources such as federal and state agencies, scholarly publications, articles, and journals should be used. Data from local colleges, universities, libraries, and regional public records can also be used. For example the statement should provide data on how the issue impacts people, the mortality rates, the number of affected families, etc., as it can go a long way in portraying a picture of the severity of the issue. In such a case giving mortality rate percentage is a better way of painting the picture than saying many people die from illness. If the scholarly data does not exist utilize internal data and or local organizational data if available. If there is absolutely no data you can access, speak about that and how your proposed initiative will bring baseline data to the forefront.

Describe Your Approach

The problem statement should show the approach you intend to take to solve the identified problem. The statement should clearly state the actions or interventions the organization will implement so as to achieve the desired outcome. There are things you should take into consideration when writing about your approach and that is how your grant application relates with the funder's mission. If the funder prioritizes food security and environmental justice, the statement should focus on how your approach will improve food security and environmental justice.

Identify the gap in the current system

Describe what is currently being done and the factors that catalyze the current state of things. This way, gaps in the current state can be identified and used to indicate an actual need for change and a more sustainable solution. Make the statement community-oriented. The justification for the problem should affirm statements that describe the gaps and how those gaps impact people. A grant proposal that saves people's lives is more convincing than one that simply hosts a single event without additional information on the gap between the current state and the desired state.

Discuss potential hurdles and give a solution

An effective problem statement needs to discuss the urgency and challenges of the proposed action. Urgency can be demonstrated by highlighting the consequences of not resolving the identified challenge as soon as possible and the long term plan as well on how you intend to manoeuvre the challenges. This increases your chances of success. If a grant application does not present a sense of urgency, funders are more likely to divert their attention to more urgent proposals.

Specify the expected outcome

Lastly, a comprehensive statement should show the desired state. Indicate the direct changes expected from the implementation of the proposed project. Use estimated statistics to define outcomes as they are more interpretable. The statement of need should state that the number of families impacted by food insecurity will decrease by 100 families as a result of the the Farm to Table Cooperative year one and 200 hundred families by year two.

Implementation Activity

Take each of the focus areas and begin to write your version of each required section. Remember in this book are only examples and I will continue to remind you to always reference your RFP/NOFO in your writing. You will hear me say this again as reading and continuously referencing the RFP/NOFO is the difference between a proposal in alignment with what the funders and the grant reviewers want to know. These sections are often scored and a rubric will guide the scoring.

CHAPTER SEVENTEEN: Objectives, Methods, and Approach
Writing your Objectives

Objectives in grant proposals are statements that describe what the project aims to achieve. They can be divided into two types: goal objectives and process objectives. Goal objectives are broad and long-term, while process objectives are specific and short-term. Examples of objectives in grant proposals are:

- **Goal Objective:** Reduce food access disparities for lower-income and underserved communities.

- **Process Objective:** Marketing outreach to 300 single mothers residents in Newark, New Jersey.

- **Goal Objective:** Expand sexual assault, stalking, domestic and dating violence prevention and education programming for all university students, including all incoming students.

- **Process Objective:** Enroll 75 Newark, New Jersey elderly residents in one or more fitness and Nutrition activities.

The ability to articulate in writing the difference between a Goal Objectives vs Process Objectives is that it also assists in understanding the type of staff and resources necessary to bring them into fruition. Elements of these objectives will be utilized in your budget narrative as it describes in essence what certain elements of your budget will go to support. Please note that you can have both process and goal objectives but they should align with goals that support achieving that is intended to be addressed by the funder.

Writing your Methods

Writing about your methods is essentially justifying why you are using the strategy you have chosen to address the problem you are seeking to solve. Choosing your method is understanding the causes and the problem or problems you attempt to resolve. Ask yourself will your method break the cycle of behavior? As was detailed in earlier chapters, research comes into play when you are able to talk about where this method has been successful? If you have implemented this before being able to cite its success or you know of other organizations or agencies who use this method before and were successful. Discuss how this method is a good fit for the people involved. For example, in the Newark SaS Farm to Table Cooperative the use of a CSA (Community Supported Agriculture) which provides the local community access to fresh healthy produce via a sponsored membership. This method has been successful in many cities with similar accessibility concerns. This method also provides the member an opportunity to engage with the organization to understand how their food is grown and access nutritious recipes for its use. In addition, through a collaboration with a Seafood Gleaning program we are able to provide fresh fish to community members as well. The CSA is considered a best practice but we have modified it to fit our community needs. Explaining this in your methods section is essential as it will show your understanding of the community you serve. In addition, articulating why this method is the right method for addressing the problem can add the substance needed to make your proposal a strong one.

Writing your Approach

To begin writing about your approach we must go back to an earlier discussion which is "What do you know about your funders mission? Why are they addressing this particular cause? Understanding this information will help you in discussing how your approach aligns to the funders mission. The funders mission is pivotal in writing a proposal that will have a high chance of getting awarded. From my experience in the grant writing space from the grant reviewer lens some writers prioritised their own mission in the rationale over that of the funder and failed to align it with the mission the funder intended to achieve. For instance, if the funder's mission is to increase literacy your approach should align to increasing literacy. Another way to think about it is simply "there are many roads to get to the city" if the goal is getting to the city then the approach should render or support that outcome.

The overall expectation of this section is to describe your understanding of your community, the strategy selected, how the strategy aligns to the alignment and outcome, and the why behind your strategy. This is where all your reflection from the beginning of the book will come to life in your writing.

Implementation Activity

Take each of the focus areas and begin to write your version of each required section. Remember in this book are only examples and I will continue to remind you to always reference your RFP/NOFO in your writing. You will hear me say this again as reading and continuously referencing the RFP/NOFO is the difference between a proposal in alignment with what the funders and the grant reviewers want to know. These sections are often scored and a rubric will guide the scoring.

CHAPTER EIGHTEEN: Understanding and Developing The Logic Model
"Logic is the beginning of wisdom, not the end."
– Leonard Nimoy

The Logic Model

Logic models are visual representations or diagrams that illustrate how a program or intervention is intended to work. For those who are new to the grant writing space hearing the word "Logis Model" can cause a little anxiety especially when you have never written one before. Some RFPs/NOFOs provide a logic model template yet may use very research heavy language to explain how it is developed. In other instances it is simply a blank template where you would have to research this on your own. The following section was written in what I hope is the most user friendly way to complete a logic model.

Components of A Logic Model

The key components of a logic model are typically organized into five main categories: inputs, activities, outputs, outcomes, and impacts.

| INPUTS | ACTIVITIES | OUTPUTS | OUTCOMES | IMPACTS |

Impacts are not as utilized in many logic model templates as a separate column and the language is written under Outcomes column under long-term effects.

A Logic Model Template

INPUTS		ACTIVITIES		OUTPUTS		OUTCOMES		
						Short-term (12 weeks)	Medium-term (6 months)	Long-term (12 months)

In some instances the Outcomes Column does not have subcategories delineated like the previous example but the same information is entered in the single Outcomes column.

The following will assist you in understanding the sections of the Logic Model.

1. **Inputs:** These are the resources, both human and material, that are invested in the

program. Inputs can include things like funding, staff time, equipment, and materials.

2. **Activities:** These are the specific actions or interventions that the program undertakes in order to achieve its objectives. Activities can include things like training, outreach, or counseling.

INPUTS

ACTIVITIES

Funding for program operations

Program staff to oversee program planning and implementation

Partnerships with local high schools and city school district

Facilities to hold college workshops and counseling sessions

Evaluation specialists to assist with program planning and develop a system for data collection and evaluation

Train staff to develop and deliver college workshops and counseling services

Recruit low-income youth attending local high schools to the program

Provide college workshops and counseling sessions

3. **Outputs:** These are the immediate products or services that result from the program's activities. Outputs can include things like the number of people trained, the number of workshops conducted, or the number of brochures distributed. Outcomes are often

divided up into three categories: Initial, intermediate, and long-term.

Program	Output (what it does)	Outcome (the change as a result)
Free medical clinic	Fifty low-income individuals are provided free doctor visits	50% decrease in emergency room visits by population served in the year following initial contact
Math tutoring program	Seventy youth receive math tutoring twice a week during the school year	100% of youth served improve their ISTEP scores in math from the start of the school year compared to the spring test
Youth mentoring	Thirty youth are matched with an adult mentor for the year	80% of youth served report increased self esteem following one year of mentoring
Dropout prevention	Forty youth at risk of dropping out receive weekly case management services	85% of youth in program for one year or longer graduate high school in four years

4. **Outcomes:** These are the changes that occur as a result of the program's outputs. Outcomes can be short-term, intermediate, or long-term and can include changes in knowledge, behavior, or attitudes.

   a. **Initial**: Change in knowledge, attitude, or skills
   b. **Intermediate**: Change in behavior or action resulting from new knowledge
   c. **Long-term**: Change in life condition and/or status

The essence of a logic model is summarizing your narrative in bullet points. It highlights a snapshot of elements that will answer **"If ... then"** from column to column.

If we implement youth mentorship.... **then** thirty youth are matched with an adult mentor.

If thirty youth are matched with an adult mentor .... **then** 80% of youth served report increased self esteem following one year of mentoring.

When it come to the Outcomes they encompass initial, intermediate, and long-term goals as depicted in the following chart:

Program	Initial Outcome (attitude)	Intermediate Outcome (behavior)	Long-term Outcome (condition)
Free medical clinic	Recipients learn how to better manage their health and where to access community resources	**50% decrease in emergency room visits by population served in the year following initial contact**	Those served have a higher quality of life and longer life expectancy
Math tutoring program	**100% of youth served improve their ISTEP scores in math from the start of the school year compared to the spring test**	90% of youth served are able to move on to the next grade	Youth graduate high school
Youth mentoring	**80% of youth served report increased self esteem following one year of mentoring**	Youth served for one year are 40% less likely to use drugs compared to their peers.	Youth avoid delinquent behaviors and become responsible citizens
Dropout prevention	100% of youth served understand the economic impact of dropping out of school	90% of youth served will advance to the next grade	**85% of youth in program for one year or longer will graduate high school in four years**

5. **Impacts:** These are the broader changes that occur as a result of the program's outcomes. Impacts can include changes in social, economic, or environmental conditions and are often difficult to measure.

By clearly identifying and mapping out each of these components, a logic model provides a clear and systematic way to understand how a program is designed to work, what resources are needed to implement it, and what outcomes and impacts it is expected to achieve.

Implementation Activity

Take each of the logic model sections and begin to write your version of each. Remember in this book these are only examples and I will continue to remind you to always reference your RFP/NOFO in your writing. You will hear me say this again as reading and continuously referencing the RFP/NOFO is the difference between a proposal in alignment with what the funders and the grant reviewers want to know. These sections are often scored and a rubric will guide the scoring.

CHAPTER NINETEEN: The Budget and The Budget Narrative

"When money realizes that it is in good hands,
it wants to stay and multiply in those hands."
– Idowu Koyenikan

The Budget

The budget is one of the most underrated requirements of the grant. It is left to the last minute it may stem from the fact that in most RFP/NOFO this is oftentimes sequentially the last part of the proposal. The budget should actually be written as you are laying out the timeline to ensure you have the necessary funding allotted to implement the activities. If you design the objectives, action plan timeline, and budget properly, your project design should flow naturally and easily. I myself have felt tense when it comes to numbers but I had to evolve that in order to support the writing of the Budget Narrative. Grant Writers have to be good with both words and numbers. To be clear you do not have to be an accountant to write a grant but you do need to understand budgets. This is written in hopes that small grassroots organizations and or teams of 3 or the Army of one can get through the budget and the budget narrative.

Similar to S.M.A.R.T. goals for objectives, the budget should be written the same manner specific, measurable, achievable, relevant, and time-bound.

Specific: To begin, list all your subcategories. Be specific when listing all your subcategories. Ex. Full-Time Employee (FTE) Project Director.

Measurable: When you go to quote a salary of cost it should break down exactly what it covers. Ex. FTE Project Director at 2080 hours x $25 per hour = $52,000.

Achievable: Your budget at all times needs to make sense. If you are saying 2080 hours, does your proposed project justify the need for available work. If there is a required training or necessary travel be sure to include the travel costs in the proper section. There are often mandatory training and conferences you have to attend within some RFP/NOFO award requirements.

Relevant: If you put your timeline next to your budget and are sure that each item is accounted for, then your budget should be relevant. The way to determine relevance is by aligning to your program design and timeline. If either is missing elements of the other then make the adjustments accordingly. Keep in mind that you need to keep in mind the amount that is directed from the specific grant.

Time-bound: Your budget should be listed from year to year in most cases. When you have a three-year grant each year should be broken down separately. There are some grants that are less than a year or for a specific amount of time and in this case you can still use the year and detail the time frame accordingly.

Now that we have identified how the budget items should be written let's look at each of the standard budget categories.

Personnel

In the personnel section you want to include the staff that will be working on the grant project. This may include positions that have not been hired yet but are necessary for the project being proposed. Ensure that for multiple years you account for possible inflation. The following is what the personnel budget line item can look like :

	Year 1	Year 2	Year 3	Total
Personnel				
Project Director 2080 x $25 hr. Yr 1 +3000 Year 2 and 3	$52,000	$55,000	$57,000	$164,000

You are not required to add the cost of inflation but it is in best practice to do so. As it pertains to personnel it is in good practice to obtain everyone's resume as well as job descriptions for positions you are intending to add.

When it comes to how much someone should be paid I usually research the national average for a position and of course look at what the grant award amount is. You can Visit https://www.dol.gov/whd/ for more information for your specific state. One of the things we keep in mind is the need to provide someone a "living wage". While some states have minimum wage requirements it is important to think about what your staff brings to the table and the monetary exchange that makes it ethical and sound.

Personnel Budget Narrative Example:

Managing Director: Newark SaS will allocate 30% of the managing director's time towards this project at $35 per hour for 2080 hours, totaling $21,840. The managing director will oversee and compile reports, and supervise the project manager, farm manager, and bookkeeper.

Fringe Benefits

Fringe benefits vary from organization to organization, except for the Federal Insurance Contributions Act (FICA) rate, which is made up of two items: Social Security and Medicare taxes. All other fringe benefits vary from state to state and from organization to organization. A cautionary note is to make sure you are following your contract and grant requirements. For instance, some state contracts may require that you include health and welfare for your employees, and they will include a specific rate. Read your contracts and make sure you incorporate all requirements.

Fringe Benefits Budget Narrative Example:

FICA: The FICA rate is at 7.65%, for $5,887.44 for grant requested salaries and $856.80 for non federal personnel salaries, totaling $6,744.24.

Travel

There are times where there are requirements for travel as a result of the grant award. In addition, travel necessary for activities written within the proposal for the proposed project. This travel should be calculated as close to the cost as possible. It is best practice to understand when traveling by plane the prices can vary depending on the seasons and or major holidays. Do not underestimate this cost as it can raise questions for the reviewer on how you will meet the requirements within the RFO/NOFO and the activities described in your submission. You should also gas mileage for using the minivan to transport participants or community resources. Be sure to review your narrative to include any staff travel or training accordingly. It is necessary to include the following in your travel calculations:

- costs of lodging
- flights or trains
- rental cars
- per diem

Go to https://www.gsa.gov/portal/content/104877 to verify your calculation for every city in the United States. It is customary that meals & Incidentals are at 75% of total daily costs when traveling to and from destination. You should utilize the IRS standard mileage rates for general driving costs. Visit the IRS website for updated information.

Travel Budget Narrative Example:

Required Training: Newark SaS will have the project manager and bookkeeper attend the required conference in Washington D.C. The current airfare price from Newark, NJ to Washington D.C. is $500. Therefore, we will have two people taking round trip flights at $1,000. Lodging, based on the GSA estimates, will be $182 per night for two people, totaling $1,092. Meals and Incidentals, based on current GSA estimates, will be $69 per day for three days for two people, plus $51.75 for two days of traveling, totaling $621. All required training costs will be grant requested at $2,713.

Equipment

This category can be a little confusing as a lot of organizations want to include computers and cellphones under this category. That might work for a foundation grant, but if you are considering federal grants, then adhere to the federal requirements. According to the Federal Uniform Guidelines in the Code of Federal Regulations, equipment is defined as:

> "tangible personal property (including information technology systems) having a useful life of more than one year and a per-unit acquisition cost which equals or exceeds the lesser of the capitalization level established by the non-federal entity for financial statement purposes, or $5,000." 2 CFR 200.33

What this basically means in laymen's terms is that any item (not separate items that surpass $5,000 when combined, but a singular item) that will be $5,000 or more and has a life span of more than one year is considered equipment. I would suggest listing at least three quotes to show that you are getting the best deal on the equipment.

Equipment Budget Narrative Example:

Minivan: Newark SaS requests the purchase of a seven-seater minivan at $20,000. The minivan is essential for driving our fresh healthy food boxes to residents and initiative participants to local farms. See three quotes of minivans to ensure the most economical cost for the minivan, totaling $20,000.

Supplies

This section is where the breakdown of your program budgets are going to help you identify these specific supply costs. It is important to note as many costs as possible. Too often small grassroots organizations are not accounting for true supply costs. These costs begin to accumulate as needed. A ream of paper can range from 5 to 10 dollars. If you know there is a lot of printing done to support the proposed initiative it is necessary to include this as after 3 months it can be a cost of 1000.00 dollars just on paper. This can include consumables, such as paper, printing costs, staples, and so forth. It can also include pamphlets and other types of costs.

Supplies Budget Narrative Example:

Consumables: Newark SaS requests $600 per year from the grant, and will provide a non federal match of $600 per year from XYZ Foundation. Consumables include paper, staples, ink, cleaning supplies, and clipboards. Consumables total $1,200 per year.

Contractual/Consultant

Contractual refers to the types of services or items that different sources are performing. This, at times, can be where you may contract an accounting agency to do your bookkeeping. If you actually contract this work, you would not include the agency as an employee in the personnel category because you are not paying their fringe benefits, and they are not employees. Please note that for some grants there are contractual vetting and guidelines that may require you to put out a solicitation for vendors and or require certain certification requirements. This requirement will be provided in writing in the RFP/NOFO.

Contractual/Consultant Budget Narrative Example:

Advertising: Newark SaS will hire an advertising contractor to create public awareness and advertisements on the television and radio for two months at $1,000 for each month, totaling $2,000.

Other

The other category is basically where you put any other anticipated expenses. I am including computers within this category, although those can also be included within supplies. This is where we would identify any items that wouldn't be classified in any other category.

Other Budget Narrative Example:

Computers: Newark SaS will purchase two computers – one for the project manager and one for the bookkeeper – to complete all programmatic and financial reports. The computers will be $1,000 each, totaling $2,000.

Venue for Nutrition: Newark SaSwill provide a space of 150 square feet valued at $100 per hour for a total of 10 hours (sessions) to discuss nutrition health. The use of this space totals $1,500.

Internet: The Internet will be required for all reports, social media posts, and administration. Internet cost is $100 per month for 12 months, totaling $1,200. We will request $600 from the grant, and $600 will be covered by a non-federal foundation grant.

Indirect Costs

If you have an indirect cost rate, then include what that is. If you do not have an indirect cost rate, I highly recommend that you include the allowed a de minimis indirect cost rate of 10%. The 10% is not too much to come off the top and can help provide support for other costs which may not be included in the project costs as they are indirect. These costs may include executive and administrative salaries (as mentioned in the personnel section), rent, utilities, and other costs that are more 'overhead' appropriate.

Indirect Budget Narrative Example:

Indirect Cost: Newark SaS will include a de minimis 10% indirect cost rate that will cover costs of utilities, executive and administrative salaries, legal fees, insurance, etc.

Please note that when grants require a match you must highlight the match in your budget and budget narrative. Not all grants require a match. When they do require a non-federal match include letters of commitment, leases, memorandums of understanding, and other required contracts to demonstrate commitment. If you are requesting an item worth more than $5,000, include at least three quotations to demonstrate the cost of the request and to show cost efficiency. In the end your budget and budget narrative will allow for a strong grant proposal submission.

Implementation Activity

Create a budget and budget narrative for your proposal. Remember in this book these are only examples and I will continue to remind you to always reference your RFP/NOFO in your writing. You will hear me say this again as reading and continuously referencing the RFP/NOFO is the difference between a proposal in alignment with what the funders and the grant reviewers want to know. These sections are often scored and a rubric will guide the scoring.

CHAPTER TWENTY: Evaluation and Reporting Management

It's objective evaluations that give our hardwiring principles teeth

and drive the organization toward results that last.

-Quint Studer

Reporting

What is reporting in grants?

A grant report is a document that tells the funder how you used their money and what outcomes resulted from their investment. Grant reporting is also sometimes called "progress reporting." Reporting frequency is often established once you are awarded the contract. For some Federal Grants the reporting requirement has been established in the RFP/NOFO. The main questions to ask yourself or identify is Who is writing and submitting the report? This should not be something you take lightly as some funders could hold the funding until the report is submitted. For federal grants there are multiple platforms used to upload the report and other supporting documents.

Reporting schedule should be tracked on personal and organizational calendars via calendar holds and invites. Include enough time to write, edit, and finalize the report. It is important that you align this to the reporting frequency. For some federal reporting there is a 90 and max 120 day for final report submission at the completion of the grant. Keep in mind that when you are reporting you want to express what is happening with the grant project. You can speak to successes, challenges, and if any goals that were identified in the proposal have been attained.

Reporting Frequency

Grant reporting is typically required on a regular basis, such as quarterly or annually. The frequency and specific requirements of grant reporting vary depending on the grantor and the type of grant.

Frequency Timeline:

- Annual - This report is completed on an annual basis at the year mark of the grant. Keep in mind that a year after funding you want to speak to implementation and growth.
- Bi-annual - This report is completed twice a year at the 6 month mark.
- Quarterly - This is completed every four months. This kind of frequency

- Monthly - This is completed at the end of each month. Some monthly reports will have a lot to highlight while others will have minimal updates depending on the activities slated for the month. This kind of reporting is frequently seen when funding is for construction projects and or certain research, market research, and other time-sensitive reporting.
- Final Report - The final report is where you write about overall achievements, challenges, future needs, program data, and goal attainment.

While the aforementioned describes some elements of what is included in reporting the actual requirements will be delineated by the funder through reporting guidance and expectations.

Program Evaluation

Program Evaluation The purpose of program evaluation is to systematically collect information about program activities and objectives, monitor progress, and to report and communicate results to network members, partners, stakeholders, and community. There are 3 main types of program evaluation:

Process evaluation: considers how the grant is delivered, whether the grant has been implemented as intended, any issues arising from implementation.

Outcome evaluation: examines how an initiative is leading to change.

Economic evaluation: measures the value for money and net social benefit of an initiative.

There are several benefits that come from doing a program evaluation. Here are some of the benefits:

- Informed Decision
- Accountability
- Enhanced Performance
- Increased Funding Opportunities

Some funders require that a program evaluation be conducted as one of the deliverables of the grant. When this is the case keep in mind the cost of having an evaluation conducted by a third party vendor or how you will navigate the evaluation process internally. In order to navigate the cost of the evaluation there are times where undergraduate and graduate students will need to complete a program evaluation as part of their coursework. This can be a fruitful collaboration as depending on the program it can be costly to conduct.

There are several resources that can guide a program evaluation when needed and will be posted at bidoism.com for your access. This is just a brief snapshot of what it is as evaluations when needed take on many, many, processes and protocols that are covered in detail. Program evaluation should be conducted after 3 consecutive delivery of the program to determine outcome. The reason I propose 3 is because you will have the data necessary to truly evaluate the program. Remember that after you complete the evaluation you should present the findings to your board and stakeholders as needed.

CHAPTER TWENTY ONE: Summary

"All they can say is …YES!"
-Jacqueleen Bido, EDD

You have come to the final chapter of this book yet this is not the end. This is where the work continues. This book is meant to go with you and grow with you as you continue to seek grant funding. This book should be used to build the capacity of others as you should not be the only one with this knowledge. Pay this forward to others in your organization or other grassroots organizations and nonprofit leaders. The work in grant is cyclical in nature; it doesn't end when the grant ends. Everyday there is a search you can conduct to seek funding for your organization and programming. The funding cycle for nonprofit leaders should be something that is discussed every 3 months. This allows you the ability to gauge what funding is going to be needed as grant funding cycles shift from year to year.

The Grant Writing Best Practice

1. Create a folder on Google Suite on your Computer and title it with the grant name and year. (Example: USDA UAIP 2023)
2. Open a blank document and title it. (Example: USDA UAIP Project Narrative)
3. Open the RFP or Log on to the submission platform and copy each of the questions.
4. Read the formatting requirements and set your document to those parameters.
5. Read each question and identify the information you have access to or the information you need to request from others. Identify who you need to email to acquire that information from. Then copy and paste the requested information as is or in your own words. Note: be specific about turnaround time and grant deadline.
6. For each section bold the section title. Next, press enter after each question in that section.
7. DO NOT WAIT to start answering questions you have the information for.
8. Set a Calendar invite for the grant one day before its deadline and several days and weeks before to manage your writing time.
9. Write to answer the question first! Then worry about editing.
10. As you receive documents and information add it to the grant folder so that it is in one place.
11. Once you have received all of your documents review and continue to complete the

Narrative and all other requirements.

12. Clean the document. This is when you reference your RFP again to make sure you have followed the formatting. Edit answers and remove the questions prompts to create a cohesive answer and above all that you answered the questions. Have others review if possible.

13. Give yourself time to submit. Copy and Paste can take longer than anticipated and you want to make sure that platform is not having technical difficulties.

14. APPLY, APPLY, APPLY!!!

15. APPLY, APPLY, APPLY!!!

16. APPLY, APPLY, APPLY!!!

17. APPLY, APPLY, APPLY!!!

18. APPLY, APPLY, APPLY!!!

19. APPLY, APPLY, APPLY!!!

20. APPLY, APPLY, APPLY!!!

21. APPLY, APPLY, APPLY!!!

RESOURCE LINKS @ BIDOISM.COM

IRS 501c3

- Council of Nonprofits Fiscal Sponsorship Infographic
- Fiscal Sponsor Directory
- https://www.fiscalsponsors.org/
- https://www.guidestar.org/search
- Fiscal Sponsorship Agreement Sample (coloradotrust.org)
- Model-A-fiscal-sponsorship-agreement-SLS-sample-08-19-20.pdf (stanford.edu)
- Applying for Tax Exempt Status Overview

Research

- USDA ERS - Publications
- Seton Hall University Dissertations and Theses (ETDs) | Seton Hall University Dissertations and Theses | Seton Hall University (shu.edu)
- Google Scholar
- Topics | USDA
- USDA Urban Agriculture Programs at a Glance (farmers.gov)
- Newark360 Master Plan | Newark360
- Transforming our world: the 2030 Agenda for Sustainable Development | Department of Economic and Social Affairs (un.org)
- Logic Model Planning Process | National Institute of Food and Agriculture
- usda.gov)Seton Hall University Dissertations and Theses (ETDs) | Seton Hall University Dissertations and Theses | Seton Hall University (shu.edu)

Data Collection

- Civil Rights Data | U.S. Department of Education
- 7 Data Collection Methods in Business Analytics (hbs.edu)
- What is a Focus Group | Step-by-Step Guide & Examples
- Data Collection Methods
- https://segment.com/blog/data-life-cycle/

Evaluation and Management

- https://www.ruralcenter.org/sites/default/files/Evaluation_Plan_Guide_Allied.pdf
- Microsoft PowerPoint - Developing an Effective Evaluation Plan.pptx

Abstract and Statement of Need

- https://your.yale.edu/sites/default/files/files/HowToWriteACompellingAbstractForGrantApplication_July2017.pdf
- HowToWriteAnAbstract_final.pdf

ABOUT THE AUTHOR
JACQUELEEN M. BIDO, EDD

A Newark, New Jersey native, Dr. Jacqueleen Bido earned her Doctorate from Seton Hall University in Educational Leadership, Management, and Policy. Dr. Bido served in Operation Iraqi Freedom and Operation Enduring Freedom during her time in the US Navy as an Information Systems Tech. As a former District Administrator for Parent and Family Engagement in the Orange County Public Schools Title I Department she coached and trained 73 Parent Engagement Liaisons and schools in implementing successful communication strategies and systems for engaging parents, families, and the community. While in the Orange County Public Schools Minority Achievement Office she focused on Males of Color, My Brother's Keeper and Find Your Voice Initiatives to impact academic and social-emotional disparities. She is the founder of Elevate Newark and BIDOISM, LLC., which are consulting companies created to empower and help people, their organizations, and the communities they serve to invoke social change. She continues to expand her mission through business consultation, program development, and grant writing to support local and national initiatives. As community collaborator and dynamic trainer she seeks to engage all stakeholders in a "Strategy for Peace of Mind."She is a mother to five beautiful children, who have been her greatest achievement because their mere existence proves the importance of the work she does to make the world a better place for them and all to live.

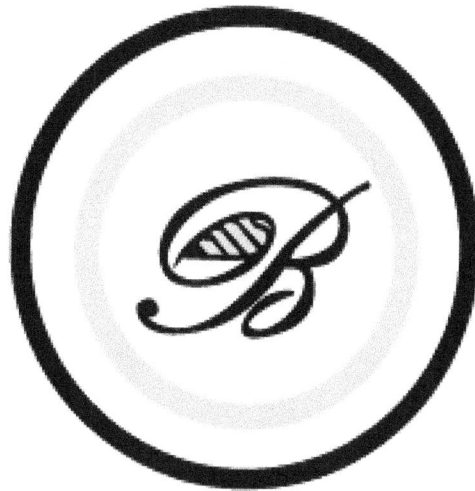

BIDOISM

A STRATEGY
FOR
PEACE OF MIND

PRAISE FOR *OUT OF THE OFFICE*

A pastor is called to be the theologian of her or his church. Accordingly, although pastors are generalists, they are also practical and pastoral theologians, whose vocations need to be guided by solid theological reflection. Bob Cornwall presents an insightful and inspirational vision of ministry for the twenty-first century, inviting pastors to become the intellectual, spiritual, and prophetic leaders of their congregations. This short and accessible book is a must-read for seminarians, seeking wisdom for the practice of ministry, and congregational and institutional pastors in need of inspiration and guidance to deepen their practice of ministry.

– Dr. Bruce Epperly
Pastor, author of
Tending to the Holy: The Practice of the Presence of God in Ministry
and *A Center in the Cyclone: Twenty-first Century Clergy Self-care*

In a time when many voices are speaking of the demise of the local congregation and the "nones" are the leading group in the "religious" sector, Robert Cornwall has boldly presented a positive word for the local congregation in his book, *Out of the Office: A Theology for Ministry*. He acknowledges the weaknesses of the local congregation, but believes that through an openness to new forms and practices of ministry that emerge through an evolving belief systems, that the local congregation still has a significant role in ministry today. He broadens the concept of the local parish to reach out into the neighborhood and the world around it in ministry that involves the local congregation, both clergy and laity drawing upon their spiritual gifts, to engage in missional activities. *Out of the Office: A Theology of Ministry* offers the professional clergy and laity a challenge to be the Church today that Jesus envisioned as a servant and missional ministry in the whole world.

– William Powell Tuck
Author of *Star Thrower: A Pastor's Handbook*
and *Stewardship: The Forgotten Beatitude*

Once again, Dr. Robert Cornwall provides the church with a valuable book. In his new book, *Out of the Office,* he tackles the important questions of what is ministry; how do we effectively engage in ministry; and what does ministry look like in our globalizing world? This prophetic work is eloquently written and beautifully reflects Dr. Cornwall's deep spirituality and faith.

– Grace Ji-Sun Kim
Associate Professor of Theology at Earlham School of Religion and author of *Embracing The Other* and *Mother Daughter Speak*

Seldom do we find careful reflection on the theology and practice of ministry that is grounded in Scripture, theology, and ecclesiastical history instead of pragmatics. Robert Cornwall, an active pastor, has provided such a work. In eighty short pages he interprets the development of ministry from the early church to the modern day. Here is a clearly written, vibrant theology of ministry and its practice. If you are in ministry of any type, you will no doubt find your vision of that ministry rekindled while reading and studying this volume.

– Jerry Gladson, Ph.D.
Senior Minister Emeritus
First Christian Church (Disciples of Christ), Marietta, GA